BOBBY J. GALLO

FAMILY SPIRITS

THE ADVENTURES AND EVIDENCE OF GALLO FAMILY GHOST HUNTERS

To my amazing and talented family who made these incredible adventures the memories of a lifetime. You are the greatest of God's blessings.

To my Dad in heaven, who's messages to me began my quest for answers.

"Not a window was broken, and the paint wasn't peeling, Not a porch step sagged, yet there was a feeling.

That beyond the door, and into the hall, This was the house, of no one at all.

No one who breathed, nor laughed, nor ate, nor said I love, nor said I hate.

Yet something walked, along the stair, Something that was, and wasn't there.

That is why weeds on the path grow high, And even the moon, races fearfully by.

For something walks, along the stair, Something that is, and isn't there."

THE HAUNTED HOUSE BY VIC CRUME

Contents

Foreword

Over the past 20 years, I've worked with hundreds of ghost hunters. Some were beginners. Others were pros.

Every one of them had a story to tell, but few shared experiences as compelling and eerie as Bobby J. Gallo's.

When I recommend a ghost hunting book, the author has to impress me. That's not just about the writing.

I look for qualities I insist upon when I assemble an investigative team.

The researcher should be intelligent. If he or she overlooks natural – if odd – explanations, that's a liability.

In addition, I want to see a balance of healthy skepticism and wide-eyed enthusiasm. Once a researcher becomes jaded or cynical, he's lost his objectivity.

Describing an investigation, the person should draw a clear line between the events as they happened, and the personal, subjective impact of what happened.

Humor is essential. If you take yourself – or ghost hunting – too seriously, investigations become tedious. You lose your credibility.

After reading this book, Bobby J. Gallo ranks high on my list of bright, down-to-earth, eager, and curious ghost hunters.

Even better, Bobby's expertise in stage magic is unbeatable. If anyone can spot a hoax or debunk something weird at a haunted site, it's Bobby. He's like a real-life version of the British TV series, *Jonathan Creek.*

In these pages, Bobby shines as a storyteller. These aren't made-up stories, but personal experiences and real ghostly encounters.

Along the way, Bobby shares tips and insights that every ghost hunter can learn from… and yes, that includes me.

Of course, many paranormal investigators write great how-to books. They explain the nuts and bolts of ghost hunting. They recommend the best equipment and how to use it. They describe how and where to find the eeriest haunts.

Other authors describe their investigations in fascinating detail. Their accounts are so compelling and authentic, even experienced ghost hunters get chills, reading their stories.

In this book, Bobby combines both talents.

From the start, he welcomes us into his family of ghost hunters. Reading this book, I felt as if I knew everyone on his team, and liked them.

Bobby's writing style is fresh and fun. His stories ring true. His illustrations show ghost hunting as it really is. He's a likable guy and generous with his insights.

But mostly, Bobby's warmth, sincerity, and humor combine to bring us into the experience. You'll feel like you're right there, as part of each ghostly encounter and investigation.

Whether you want to become a ghost hunter or read creepy (but true) ghost stories on dark and stormy nights – or both – I think you'll enjoy this book.

Fiona Broome
Author and Paranormal Researcher

Preface

In the past ten years, the paranormal phenomenon fueled by the popularity of ghost hunting television shows has taken the world by storm. People from all walks of life. Every background, ethnicity, political persuasion, and age have become borderline obsessed with this incredibly controversial subject. A community almost as diverse as the reasons they become involved in the first place.

Some are looking for enlightenment. Some are looking for proof of life after death. And still others become involved for the sake of debunking it all.

Paranormal groups have become widespread and exist in every country and on every continent across the globe. There are even individuals and companies who's sole focus is the development of cutting edge electronic instruments and phone apps for the singular purpose of attempting to contact the dead.

And that's where we come in… *Gallo Family Ghost Hunters - G.F.G.H* have become an underground phenomenon in the paranormal community earning tens of thousands of views on our award winning webseries. The adventures we have experienced were, and continue to be amazing. And even though it's easy just to watch our entertaining episodes, there is so much to be said about what happened behind the scenes, and why certain moments were so significant… And sometimes frightening.

These experiences have also given us a definite perspective of the paranormal field and what we consider valid evidence and methods. Interspersed between the discussion of episodes, we will be talking about our views and the views of others when it comes to all things paranormal. Our equipment will also be analyzed. Why we use it, and why we believe it works. As well as exclusive background stories which have never been revealed until now.

Chances are, if you are a parapsychologist, paranormal investigator, or fellow ghost hunter, you probably won't agree with some of our methodology or validity of evidence. In fact, I have never run into two people in our field who believe in exactly the same things. That's the price of being a pioneer. We are literally sailing across a sea that has no land in sight...Yet. So this book is predominately written based upon our own methods and experiences with the exception of some key informational sources we used as a guide and are listed at the end of this book on the recommended resources page.

It is my sincere hope that the reader approaches this work with an open mind, and reads the book until it's completion despite any possible preconceived notions about certain aspects of the content.

There are no experts in the world of the paranormal. And to this day, no solid scientific proof of ghosts. However, there are mountains of evidence and personal experience. So much so that millions across the planet continue to pursue this extraordinary challenge... Including us.

Bobby J. Gallo

Acknowledgement

My incredible family, Renee, Nicolet, and Courtnee without whom, none of this would have been possible.

My wonderful mom for putting up with my strangeness from magic, to the rock band, then back to the magic again… Supporting me every step of the way, even though she would much rather I was an accountant.

My brother Vince who must still think I'm weird. But hey, that's what brothers are for. Also his wife Jill who relayed that life-changing message to me from my late father.

To the late Dr. Harry Stafford, our first mentor in the paranormal field.

Fiona Broome, for writing the foreword to this book and providing her expert advice when needed.

April Abercrombie of Ghost Advice for writing the afterword to the book and keeping me grounded with alternate viewpoints during some pretty intense debates on Facebook.

Walter Fritz, my high school drama teacher and play director. The skills you taught me I've used my entire life and eventually brought me here… Thank you.

All of my paranormal friends and colleagues including: Lance Philip of EKG , Mollie Abramitis, John and Debbie Holliday, Chuck Gotski, Reverend Neil Farley, Hugh Fairman, Brigid Mcdermott Goode and Pamela Spicknall of The Ghost Gals, Jamie Pearce of Historic Haunts, Daniel Roberge of Big Beard Studios, Scott Krug of Krugism Development LLC, Hope Sargent, Anthony Ortiz, Chickie Haute, Jane Horton Starr, Robert Grote, Virgil Colligan from ECRIPT (East Coast Research, Investigation, and Development Team), Kirsten Klang of Mystical Minnesota Paranormal, Nicole Novelle, and Cyrus Kirkpatrick.

Also a special thank you to: GTN, DailyMotion, Blip.TV, Vimeo, The International Conservatory of Magic Online, Steve Fredericks of The Growing Stage at The Palace Theater, The Salem Inn, Asheville Masonic Temple, Millie of Historic Rosedale Plantation, Rose Bean Schledwitz of Times Past Haunted Farm, The Spratt family, Paranormal Kool-Aid Radio, Paranormal King Radio, and the Ad Twins.

Also to my showbiz friends: Bill Wisch, Dan and Gerri Abrahamsen of DCA Productions, Mickey "Who?" Loesch, Wanda Ellett, Laurie Wheatman Zoock, The PSY-GUYS: Mike Emma, Shawn Bates, and Brian J Orlowski, The rock band ARSENAL: Bob Nunn, Mike Lemire, Rob Cole, with Martin Olivo on lights (they were truly paranormal), and the late Lou Batson.

If I missed anyone here, my apologies… But please know that you are appreciated.

Last but certainly not least… William, Malcolm, Jenny, Lou, Nancy, Catherine, Emma, Thomas, Acton, Mary Elizabeth, Annie, Matilda, Susannah, Sophia, Captain Nathaniel West, and all of the other ghosts who have interacted with us throughout this fascinating adventure… You have not been forgotten.

1

Gallo Family Ghost Hunters

T hank you for purchasing this book and allowing our ghost hunting adventures into your world. We are a regular, All-American family who is normal in every way except one. We talk to ghosts. Yea, for real…

From the outset, we have to make this essential disclaimer. We may be an unlikely band of ghost hunters. And many will see this picture and say, *"if they can do it, so can we."* But this hobby isn't for everyone. If you follow in our footsteps and set out to contact supernatural entities using any or all of the methods described in this book, you do so at your own risk. This isn't a game. And since you will see my kids engaging in these activities it must be stressed that children should never ghost hunt unless supervised and guided by a parent knowledgeable in the study of the paranormal. *This is for real.* To that end some will scoff at that statement while others will take it "dead" seriously. But at the end of the day, it's your choice and sole responsibility.

But before we delve into the unknown and permanently change the way you view the supernatural forever, we have a little ghostly housekeeping to do. I think it's appropriate to offer a short biography of each team member so that you can get to know us on a more personal level and see our perspective on the paranormal. Perhaps you will see similarities with yourself and your own family?

Gallo Family Ghost Hunters

Bobby J.

My fascination with ghosts began way back in my childhood. Other than comics and superheros, my favorite hobby was collecting all things monster related. Favorite shows included; *Chiller* and *Creature*

Feature on Saturday nights while *Famous Monsters of Filmland* was my dream magazine. I can still envision the six fingered hand rising out of a pool of blood with the dead tree in the background, while a creepy voice echoed *"Chilllerrrr."* And let us not forget the daytime drama *Dark Shadows.* The show where I waited and agonized for Barnabas Collins to show his fangs. An event which happened maybe once every hundred episodes or thereabouts! So unfair.

I was the nerdy kid who always tried to scare my cousins and friends with rubber monster masks, plastic fangs, and most memorably, my mom with a latex appendage called *The Spook Hand* that would stick out of a closet door, or wherever you wanted to place it. When everyone else my age was listening to the *Bay City Rollers*, my favorite record was the sound score to the 1950's supernatural series *One Step Beyond.* Yea, I was weird.

I also remember having strange dreams about the paranormal as a child. Two stand out as particularly frightening. So much so that I remember them in detail to this day.

In the first dream, there was an old stone church on Maple ave. in Netcong NJ where the municipal building now stands. It was Baptist I believe and built sometime in the mid to late 1800's. In my dream, I remember standing in front of the old wooden arched doors when suddenly, they swung open revealing only darkness. As I foolishly entered, I remember the floor beginning to move much like a conveyor belt. I then remember falling backwards onto my back as I was being pulled into the blackness by the moving floor with nothing but laughter echoing around me. Then I woke up, thank God.

In the other dream, I found, for some inexplicable reason, that I was the only one left on the planet. As I searched up and down my street and the neighboring street. All I could hear was a loudspeaker warning everyone to get indoors (so that's where they all went!) because a maniac was on the loose. Suddenly, I could see him in the distance, walking towards me; a dark overcoat, with a very wide brimmed hat pulled down low so you couldn't see his face. No matter how fast I ran, I would look back and there he was, ever so much closer, still walking while I ran, but he was catching up. *Closer... Closer... Closer...* My fault for watching *Ray Miland* in the classic horror movie, *The Man With The X-Ray Eyes* before bed-time.

In all seriousness though, I later found out that the man in my dream may have been the infamous *Hat Man*. A terrifying shadow person so many others have experienced. Accounts and drawings of him certainly do match the memory of the man from my dream.

I couldn't care less about sports, my parents had to force me to play little league. Even when I became a budding magician, a past-time that I would eventually parlay into a full-time career, I always gravitated toward the spookier, *Bizarre* type of magic. I can still remember reading a book entitled *Houdini on Magic* which I borrowed from my elementary school library. In it I saw a reproduction of an old Houdini promotional poster that read: *Do Spirits Exist?*, Houdini says *"No!" and proves it!* As a bizarre kid I was mortified! *"I thought Houdini was supposed to do the opposite! ... He needs to convince people that they DO exist! ... After all, isn't that the job of a magician?"* Or so I thought.

What I didn't know at the time, and would have learned had I not just skipped to the magic trick sections instead of reading the entire book. Is that Houdini was a staunch skeptic of the *Victorian Spiritualist* movement of that time period birthed by the famous *Fox Sisters* of Rochester New York. Houdini thought people were getting taken advantage of by false mediums at the time. Whether or not this was or was not the case is still the subject of fierce debate.

4

On the flip-side, the skeptic movement has grown in a different direction entirely. People like James Randi, an ex-magician who fancies himself a "paranormal expert" (ironic since you really can't be an expert on something you don't believe in) has devoted his life to debunking every aspect of the paranormal, but I digress.

As I grew older and into high school my interest in magic and monsters faded, while dreams of becoming a rock star took center stage. Heavily influenced by KISS, our band was actually quite ahead of it's time for the high-school garage variety. We had flash pots, dry ice smoke machines, the works! Great memories and concerts that people talk about to this day. No lie, people who were at these performances in the early 80's are still asking us if we are ever going to have a reunion. But life happens and those dreams have faded. For me however, performing onstage was still in the cards, literally.

Several years later I found myself working as a full-time professional magician performing 300-400 shows per year. Touring the college circuit and being represented by the prestigious theatrical agency, *DCA productions in NYC*, which also represented famous celebrities such as Jeff Dunham and *Saturday Night Live* cast members. I performed all across America, and even appeared on television a number of times. In fact, I held the record for most appearances on the regional television show, *Jersey's Talking* with the legendary talk-show host and sportscaster, Lee Leonard.

It was also during that time I had one of my first memorable paranormal experiences which I wrote about once before. So rather than starting from scratch, I have included the original article here. Reprinted without changes of any kind, and with expressed permission from the *Secret Passageway Forum of the International Conservatory of Magic Online at:* www.magicschool.com. The world's first and largest online school for magicians which I created in the early 90s with the help of famed sleight of hand artist Bill Wisch. The school has taught students from across the globe how to become a performing magician.

September 1997

Strange Vibrations

A True Story by Bobby J. Gallo

Many of you may know that I just got back from a college tour up and down the east coast. It was a great string of events with an interesting experience happening to me at one particular date. The school where I performed my full evening show entitled *"Sharing The Spotlight With You"* was situated in upper New England. It was a rural college with great students who showed me wonderful hospitality. Before the show I was given an old *skeleton key* to my sleeping accommodations. It was the oldest building on campus. Over 180 years old (and smelled like it!). It was originally the main school building many, many, years ago, but now served as a campus guest house and in that capacity, only used on certain special occasions. Such as visiting performers and faculty (lucky me!?). When I first arrived, I noticed that in the *Great Room* of the old mansion, there were old paintings of various people from all eras of American history. These people had something to do with the school in one way or another during their lives. But now all were long gone and their images were ~~entombed~~, umm… I mean enshrined in this ancient parlor.

As I entered the house and proceeded upstairs to my guest room accommodations, the strangest feeling came over me. The hair on the back of my neck began to stand on end for reasons I really couldn't understand at the time. I joked to myself about the place being haunted because of the age of the building coupled with the fact that

6

the room with the portraits downstairs looked like something out of *The Haunted Mansion in Disney World*. Also, the fact that I was the only one staying the night in this old mansion fueled this humorous notion.

That evening as I dressed in my finest performing attire and proceeded to the theater, where I met and began a conversation with my contact at the school before the show. I joked with her about the house and the fact that it looked like it could be haunted. She replied, *"you mean you heard about that place?"*... Stunned, I turned to her and replied back with a single word... *"WHAT?"*

It just so happens that dozens of people have experienced supernatural happenings in that old stately manor. Everyone from campus security guards to students and faculty have reported the strange ghost of a woman. My contact told me not to worry because she was supposedly a *"friendly spirit!"* However, another student contact told me to *"be afraid, be very afraid"* in what I thought was a joking tone of voice. Was I? Suffice to say that after the performance, I calmly and quietly went back into the old mansion, up the creaky wooden stairs to my room, packed my things and drove all night back home to New Jersey. It was the last gig on my tour and the drive was about 6 1/2 hours. I know that I could have checked into a hotel, but at that point it was difficult to sleep!

End of article:

In hindsight from a paranormal investigator's perspective, this experience was significant because at the time I wasn't looking for an experience. It just happened. So for that reason alone I attach validity to it. Plus, I did not want to drive through the night and would have welcomed a good night's sleep!

Also, I can still remember (and feel) the extremely heavy atmosphere in the mansion. The energy was so thick you could cut it with a knife. I had a knot in my stomach that I couldn't explain and the hair on the back of my neck was standing straight up as I wrote about in the above article. It's a common feeling many sensitive investigators experience at haunted locations. But at the time I knew none of this. Now I'm almost certain that the location was indeed haunted. Too bad I didn't have my equipment back then. If this happened to me today, you can rest assured I would have stayed the entire night and attempted to gather as much evidence as possible!

The positive thing about this experience is the fact that it paved the way for my very first paranormal investigation a very short time afterwards.

Background on the rest of the team

To say that I am proud of my wife and kids would be an understatement. They have impressed me in so many ways it's truly hard to fathom. Smart, fearless, strong, and talented would be a few words that come to mind. They are truly naturals at this game. Following are some short bios so you can get a feel for their individual personalities.

The Hidden Grave Of Thomas Sprot

Renee

Renee always had a strong religious faith and belief that there were unseen forces at work in our lives. It wasn't long after we started investigating that she realized she had certain gifts for this type of work. The type of gifts that were to blow away seasoned veterans in the field of paranormal research once they viewed our videos. Renee is an empath, and a natural born dowser. The truth is, despite my ringmaster personality and experience as an entertainer, she truly is the most talented person on the team. Though with her humble personality, she would be the first to deny it.

This is what Renee had to say concerning her involvement with Gallo Family Ghost Hunters:

"I have experienced the unexplained my entire life. I have always felt the need to look over my shoulder and have many personal experiences. Probably more so than most people. So the paranormal field has always intrigued me as somewhere I could find answers.

Other than that, I appreciated the historical and educational aspect of conducting an investigation. The background work as well as the production was always a learning experience. When people questioned me as to why I would let my kids ghost hunt, I would always point to the educational aspects of paranormal investigation. It also gives them a sense of empowerment and the knowledge that there is nothing to fear from what we suspect are ghosts.

We have had enough unfortunate experiences with spirits to come to the understanding that it is crucially important to appreciate life while we are in this physical form. So many aspects of life come into focus when you are dealing with a spirit who cannot let go of anger, or is somehow trapped here and doesn't know how to move on, or cannot. Petty squabbles and bickering in life seem insignificant when compared to the torment that may be experienced by an earthbound spirit.

My favorite episode is "Flowers For Emma," investigations like this particular one makes you feel good inside knowing that you can still do good deeds and acts of kindness, even when a person is now in spirit. When they connect and communicate with you, it makes you think, "Are they lonely?" And if they are, how wonderful is it that we can offer them a gesture of love."

Laughter At Old Burying Point

Nicky G.

The kids were rather young when we started to investigate, so their experience is obviously limited. Nicky G. though is a chip off the old block as far as her interests are concerned. Her fascination with the supernatural was evident when she had me take her to a *Twilight* convention in Charlotte NC during her teenage "goth phase" where I was the only father there. But it was fun and we even made the local newspapers because of the novelty of a dad taking his kid to meet and greet the Twilight stars.

She quickly grew out of that and became ROTC at her local high school. Smart, beautiful, and witty, she is now a licenced Cosmetologist, but still passionate about producing Gallo Family Ghost Hunters episodes. When Nicky G. was asked about her views on the paranormal, this was her response.

"I've been interested in the paranormal for as long as I can remember. When I was younger, I loved dressing up as supernatural creatures such as vampires every year. I think that deep down I secretly wanted to be one myself. While most little girls aspire to be a doctor or a ballerina, I wanted to be one of the undead! LOL. So when my dad talked about ghost hunting like they did in "Ghost Adventures" I couldn't be more excited! The aspect which made the idea even better was the prospect of doing it together as a family. I've always felt very close to them and this experience has made us even closer, so cool.

I will always look back at this part of my life and smile when I remember the awesome adventures we had (with hopefully more to come). I think in many aspects, it's when we were closest. Depending on one another and having each other's back.

I'm often asked, that if I had one superpower, what would it be? The truth is, I already have one, my intuition. I can sense emotions in both the living and the dead. I can also tell when something is not quite right. There are many examples during our investigations where it clearly came in handy. One episode which is discussed in this book immediately comes to mind, "The Gate Keeper." From the moment I stepped into that cemetery, I could feel dark and frightening energy. It was the only time I felt that we were threatened in any way during an investigation. But all we can do is chalk it up as a learning experience and move forward. It's the only direction we have."

Laughter At Old Burying Point

Courtnee

Miss personality herself. The adorable ghost-magnet who steals the show in every episode she appears in. One thing most people immediately notice about Courtnee is that she is utterly fearless. If you don't watch her like a hawk, she will be off wandering alone in a dark cemetery looking for ghosts, and is intent on finding them. Which frankly is the primary reason I purchased walkie-talkies for the team!

Though Courtnee has blossomed into a beautiful young woman as of the writing of this book, she has maintained that amazing personality and ability to capture attention. Currently a political science major at Northhampton College.

In Courtnee's own words…

"I am a fun outgoing person. My dad loves to call me "Miss Personality" because growing up I loved the spotlight. Also, it is true that people say I am "fearless." That fact is only partially true, I'm just not afraid of the paranormal (most of the time). I think everyone, no matter how brave they appear, gets freaked out now and then. Especially when you are ghost hunting. Because you really don't know what to expect. And what you don't expect, is what usually happens.

If I'm not looking for paranormal activity, you can find me at the pool (inside or out) due to my love for competitive swimming. I am currently studying political science and want to work in the government in some capacity. It may sound self-serving, but one thing that made me want to do the paranormal show growing up was the prospect of fame. Like any little girl, I wanted to be rich and famous. But over the years that has all changed. After communicating with so many ghosts, my interest in the paranormal has grown into a much more intellectual pursuit. What consumes me now is answering the one, great unsolved question, "Where do we go after death?" That is the mystery that draws me back to the paranormal, again and again. Now, not that many people believe in the paranormal. Many do, and equally as many don't. But regardless of your beliefs, don't you want to know too?"

2

What Is A Ghost?

Most paranormal enthusiasts will tell you a ghost is one of three things; the spirit, soul, or essence of a deceased human being or animal. Which is pretty self-explanatory. A residual haunt, where events happened that were so traumatic (or dramatic), such as a battlefield, that the energy expended is literally absorbed into the surroundings. It then periodically plays back like a tape loop or broken record. These hauntings are not intelligent like a human spirit. But seem to be very common in certain locations. Or something else entirely, such as, an angel, demon, shadow person, or alien.

The majority of people go with the first description. And except for a few residual haunt experiences which will be covered later, that is what we believe we were dealing with in the vast number of cases.

There are also cryptozoological creatures such as Bigfoot, Loch Ness Monster, Jersey Devil, UFO's etc. which are also considered paranormal in a broad sense. But we won't be discussing them in this book.

The Brown Lady of Raynham Hall, One of the first and most famous ghost photos of all time. Widely considered authentic "Dorothy" Lady Walpole is seen here descending the stairs.

Do ghosts really exist?

Yes, ghosts exist. And I am going to write from the perspective that they do. The evidence we and others have gathered over the years is too overwhelming to come to any other conclusion. Plus, we've communicated with enough of them through as many methods to confirm our deductions. So for us there is no longer any doubt. But why are they here?

Many religions will advocate for what I call, *the cosmic vacuum cleaner theory.* This is when one of two things happen when a person dies. They either get sucked up, or down; no in-between. Said spirit has no choice in the matter. And once you are in either place, you can't come back for any reason. Which would mean by default, that any intelligent entity a ghost hunter runs into must be in the "something else" category. However, NDE accounts (near death experiences), ADC (after life communication), and the experience of many gifted psychics show that ghosts do indeed come back from the great beyond when they desire (or get permission). Such as loved ones escorting the deceased into a tunnel of light, speaking through a medium to convey a personal message, sending signs, etc.

However, some spirits refuse (or cannot) to go into the light all together. We call these *earthbound spirits.* The reason they are earthbound can be any number of things. The most popular theory being *unfinished business.* For instance, there was someone they wanted to relay a message to, something they wanted to accomplish but never did, or they may just love the place where they lived while they still had a beating heart and don't want to leave. On the darker flip-side, perhaps they don't know that they are dead, they are trapped here by design of a higher power, they simply don't know how to proceed to *the light,* or are afraid to.

These are just a few of the great unanswered questions all ghost hunters try to find answers to, including us.

Ghosts across time

Spirits and the afterlife are two subjects that have spanned every country, culture, civilization, tribe, religion, in every age and time since the dawn of mankind. Groups of humans, with little or no contact with each other, often in opposite corners of the globe, have all acknowledged the existence of spirits. Specifics may be different, but the basic concept has always been the same. In fact, it would be no surprise at all if we found that even neanderthal and cro-magnon man (early modern humans) had this same innate knowledge that the consciousness survives death. And that spirit beings existed in their primitive understanding of a parallel dimension.

After all, we do know that primitive man buried their dead with some ceremony by including personal items such as tools and weapons (which were quite valuable at the time). So it stands to reason that they believed the departed may need them in the afterlife.

So at this early stage we already have our very first piece of afterlife evidence, *Innate knowledge*. How is it that every culture in the human species all agree on this one subject while disagreeing on virtually everything else? And I do mean everything.

Where could this idea have possibly started? What ancient wisdom was so embedded into man's psyche from the beginning, that all of these civilizations inherently knew beyond the shadow of a doubt, that the *dead never really die?* From the Ancient Egyptian, to the American Indian, to the Shintoist, to the Celtic Pagan, to the Roman

Catholic, and every group in between. All believe, with assurance, that some aspect of the human condition does not perish when the body ceases to function.

Secular psychologists speculate the reason for this belief to be the innate fear of death. However, that is far too simplistic an explanation for this universal belief as the parallels across the span of human existence are too similar and consistent. If humans as a species are all prone to this same innate belief; then perhaps instead of this spiritual knowledge being a defense mechanism of sorts, perhaps instead, they all merely recognize consciousnesses survival as being the one universal and undeniable truism.

It's only been in the past 200 years or so that a good number of academic scientists (the loud ones anyway) have abandoned any notion of an afterlife reality unless they can physically see, hear, touch, or put it in a petri dish. This is despite the hard fact that humans, though having superior intellect, have eyesight, hearing, and most other senses, inferior to that of many other species on the planet. We have learned that these "inferior" species (dogs, cats, birds etc.) routinely sense things that we cannot. And yet, materialists (a term coined for these skeptics) will often scoff at the things they cannot see or sense themselves. Ironic, to say the least.

Textbook answers that materialists have contrived to discount the existence of the afterlife and it's inhabitants never seem to take into account the countless number of times across millennia that certain amorphous energies have made contact with the living in any number of mysterious and unexpected ways. They ignore the sheer statistics which in and of themselves could be considered conclusive evidence.

Little known haunts versus paranormal attractions

I've done interviews on dozens of paranormal radio shows. And more times than not, the interviewer will ask me if we have been to the *Stanley Hotel, Waverly Hills Sanatorium, The Villisca Axe Murder House, Pennhurst Asylum, The Queen Mary,* or whatever the paranormal attraction du jour is.

The truth is, while we will at times visit infamous haunted locations such as the *Castillo de San Marcos,* more times than not, we would rather seek out unknown or little known locations that haven't been investigated to death (pun intended). After all, as I discussed with John and Debbie Holliday on their *Paranormal King* radio show, if ghosts aren't mindless energy walking around in a stupor and are as intelligent as we think they are, they must get sick of all the investigators at some of these places. Wouldn't you?

Ghosts have a story to tell, or they wouldn't have stayed behind. And it's in small, almost forgotten cemeteries like the ones we investigate, and old structures where no known haunts have been recorded where they are more likely to communicate in our opinion.

Does ghost hunting jive with organized religion?

It depends on who you are speaking with and what particular doctrine a denomination subscribes to. For instance, *The Spiritualist Church* advocates and practices afterlife communication in arguably it's purest form, which is *direct contact* via mediumship. However, a great many evangelical Christians have the polar opposite view. These well intentioned individuals will tell you that nearly everything we contact is demonic by nature (remember the cosmic vacuum cleaner theory?). They will point to verses in the old testament as the case against ghost hunting, specifically Leviticus 19:31 NIV.

"Do not turn to mediums or seek out spiritists, for you will be defiled by them."

While this obviously says what it says; it must also be pointed out that we can only speculate what was going on in the ancient pagan cultures who practiced various forms of clairvoyance. In my view, this biblical reference was more akin to the darker practice of necromancy than any modern day psychic or medium.

I remember years ago there was a popular medium in Hackettstown NJ by the name of Ginya. When you entered her house you were immediately struck by the fact that she was a devout Roman Catholic. Pictures of John Paul II and the saints adorned every wall. She actually described Renee in detail during a reading I sat for. The same woman who I would eventually meet and marry. Doesn't seem so evil to me.

I personally know several men of the cloth who are paranormal investigators including a Bishop in the *Old Catholic Church.* I have regular conversations with these men and we agree on many things. None of them are telling us not to conduct investigations. In fact, religion and faith also point out that *we must seek God.* My personal view is that by seeking evidence of the afterlife, we are by extension seeking the very nature of God. And yes, I am quite familiar with the biblical verse: John 20:29 which says,

"Then Jesus told him, "Because you have seen me, you have believed; blessed are those who have not seen and yet have believed."

And that has worked for millions upon millions of people for the past

2000 years. But for myself and others like myself, it would be nice to have a little validation. Curiosity is a God-given trait in and of itself; one that some of us exercise more than others it seems.

The *good news* for us church going ghost hunters is that a fairly recent EWTN article stated that the Vatican actually supports EVP (electronic voice phenomenon) research as long as it is done in the vein of scientific research. Here are some excerpts from this outstanding article. The first was from the Pontiff himself after several priests caught an unexpected EVP on tape,

"The existence of this voice (EVP) is strictly a scientific fact and has nothing to do with spiritism. The recorder is totally objective. It receives and records only sound waves from wherever they come. This experiment may perhaps become the cornerstone for a building for scientific studies which will strengthen people's faith in a hereafter (Italian Journal Astra, June 1990 quoted Kubis and Macy, 1995: 102)."

Also from the article,

*"The Church realizes that she cannot control the evolution of science. Here we are dealing with a scientific phenomenon; this is progress and the Church is progressive. I am happy to see that representatives of most Churches have adopted the same attitude as we have: we recognize that the subject of the Voice Phenomena stirs the imagination even of those who have always maintained that there could never be any proof or basis for discussion on the question of life after death. This book and the subsequent experiments raise serious doubts, even in the minds of atheists. **This alone is a good reason for the Church supporting the experiments.** A second reason may be found in the greater flexibility of the Church since Vatican II, we are willing to keep an open mind on all matters which do not contradict Christ's teaching (Bander 1973:103)."*

Father Gino Concetti, one of the most competent theologians in the Vatican, said in an interview:

"According to the modern catechism, God allows our dear departed persons who live in an ultra-terrestrial dimension, to send messages to guide us in certain difficult moments of our lives. **The Church has decided not to forbid any more the dialogue with the deceased with the condition that these contacts are carried out with a serious religious and scientific purpose** *(printed in the Vatican newspaper Osservatore Romano—cited in Sarah Estep's American Association Electronic Voice Phenomena, Inc Newsletter, vol 16 No, 2 1997"*

The article goes on to give numerous examples as to why paranormal research should not be prohibited, but rather encouraged to a degree. However, the church does echo my belief that care must be taken because these are "murky waters" which I contend are the *precautionary reasons* why many religions attempt to steer people away from this pursuit.

The fact is, we never have 100% certainty of what we are dealing with. That being the case, maybe it's better not to investigate the paranormal at all? Perhaps for some! But no matter what we do in life we will experience risk. Driving a car, swimming in a pool, playing sports, eating a chili dog; life is full of risks. The best we can do is take every precaution we can and make life the adventure and learning experience it was meant to be.

Finally, I can see where organized religion could be a bit apprehensive when it comes to a pursuit which may provide answers to the age old questions of life, death, and the hereafter. Especially when religion feels that this subject is it's primary job, not the job of an EMF detector or EVP recorder. I can fully appreciate and understand that, but there will always be a need for these age-old institutions. Speaking for myself, no amount of ghost hunting will ever replace the church, it's teachings, and the spiritual foundation that it offers.

Ghostly communication methods

The next few paragraphs are going to get very metaphysical and even a little *New Age*. Trust me, we will get back to the classic ghost hunting in just a moment.

For thousands of years, there have been three basic ways ghosts have communicated with the living when they could through such means as;

1. Psychics and mediums (seance)
2. Various methods of sending signs and personal experience (ADC)
3. Apparitions, sounds, and related phenomena (manifestation)

So as you can see, what we do is nothing new. It's merely another way to approach an age old fascination with the unknown. In fact, it's my contention that modern day ghost hunting did not begin with the popular TV shows of today. Ghost hunting actually began in the darkened, velvet draped parlors of the Victorian era. Yes, the classic *seance* was the forerunner of the modern day ghost hunt. And if you look at the two closely, the similarities are striking. Both use similar methodologies. Even old school tools such as Ouija boards and pendulums which were used in those sessions so many years ago, are still in use today.

Also, manifestations that have taken place in these sessions a century and a half ago, such as the appearance of *ectoplasm*, is something we still experience in various forms. So perhaps those old photos of mediums producing these ethereal materials has some basis in fact after all. That being said, since those times in the late 1800's and early 20th century, contrary to the endless scrutiny the spiritualist movement has received, it continues to this day and thrives in places like Lilydale near Rochester NY.

It's also important to note that luminaries of the Victorian era such as *Sir Arthur Conan Doyle*, author of the famous Sherlock Holmes series, and even *Mary Todd Lincoln*, wife of the 16th President of the United States, were advocates and firm believers in the Spiritualist movement; which held the classic seance as it's primary tool of afterlife communication.

I myself actually had several personal experiences where I believe I was sent messages from my departed father. These experiences fueled my personal desire to learn more about the paranormal. Here is a brief synopsis, so you can see where my head is at here.

My sister-in-law Jill was several states away from me at the time she visited a medium who asked her to relay a message to me from my dad who passed away in 1983. It was personal so I am not going to go into it here. Suffice to say that it blew me away. It was information that no one could have possibly known except for me. Yet here was the answer to a question that was plaguing me for a very long time.

Then there was a time when I was in a state of personal distress and looking for answers. Just then a sign came to me in the form of a large *monarch butterfly* which landed on my arm. I took it as a sign from my father that he was there comforting me, and that things would be okay.

"What does a butterfly have to do with ghosts and spirits you may ask?" An experience like this is known as an *After Death Communication (ADC),*

and can take on many forms.

The ways in which an ADC can happen are almost limitless. But some ways are more common than others. These communications manifest mostly through signs that are sent to us through unusual circumstances as well as certain types of creatures. Cardinals are well known for this, and yes, monarch butterflies as well. There is actually an old Irish proverb which states: *"Butterflies are the souls of the dead waiting to pass through purgatory."*

This is a phenomenon which has been studied through thousands of cases. In fact, entire books have been written about this type of occurrence and are readily available to anyone looking to research how signs are sent from beyond.

My ghost hunting daughter, Nicky G. whenever she sees a monarch butterfly says to this day, *"There goes Grandpa!"* ... And BTW, she starting doing this before she knew anything about ADC's.

It's just one of those things that most people will never believe until it happens to them. Personal experience is often called *the best teacher* as well as *the best evidence,* I wholeheartedly agree. However, many skeptics will say that this theory is just wishful thinking, or a psychological mechanism to cope with grief, yada, yada, yada, and that this is all taken on faith alone. I don't think so. Many times things happen in our lives that are *far too coincidental.* To look at it from a more logical perspective, put yourself in the ethereal shoes of the spirit. If you had to communicate a personal message to your loved one from beyond, and had no physical body to speak of, how would *you* do it?

Ghost hunting etiquette

As I have stated, we have appeared on dozens of radio programs and another one of the questions I frequently get asked so many times is, *"what do I think of those who use the antagonistic tactic of baiting a spirit into communication?"* You often see this on some of the more popular paranormal television shows.

We have always maintained that we are attempting to communicate with people. They may be dead, but they are people nonetheless and deserve our respect. Furthermore, I think our positive attitude is exactly the reason we get so much evidence. The spirits want to connect with our positivism, and they know we will not abuse them. *"How in the world could you possibly abuse a ghost you may ask?"* Well, think about it, if this is all about psychic phenomena, our thoughts may be powerful things to the spirit world. Stay focused, positive, and respectful at all times.

How can you protect yourself from nasty ghosts?

I'm going to talk about this *very important subject* now instead of later. First off, it's vitally important to stress that at the end of the day, we really don't know what we are dealing with. We believe these entities are the spirits of the dead, but no one will ever be 100% sure until we are one ourselves. That being the case, it's vitally important that one takes spiritual precautions before a ghost hunt to ensure that *nothing follows you home* from an investigation. And even if these entities are indeed the ghosts of the dearly departed, remember what was written above concerning *earthbound spirits?* They are earthbound for a reason. Sometimes for benign reasons, sometimes not.

So what can you do? Well being Catholic ourselves we opt for Catholic modes of protection (your modes may differ). After a few negative experiences I've had over the years, I no longer investigate without a *Medal of St. Benedict* on my person, or in my gear bag. Known as *the devil chasing medal* for hundreds of years, it's considered to be one of the best wards against the darker forces in existence. I now insist that everyone in my family carry one as well.

It has also been used by Anglicans, Lutherans, Methodists and the Western Orthodox, in the Benedictine Christian tradition.

I've actually considered getting this tattooed on my arm... Seriously!

Some will cleanse themselves and their gear with salt after an
investigation, others say various personal prayers and meditations

for protection. Some smudge with white sage. There are many ways depending upon your spiritual understanding.

Some are also lucky to have automatic protection, such as Courtnee. While in Salem Mass., her and Nicky G. had readings from a real Salem witch who actually told her that she was under the protection of St. Michael himself. WOW! You can't get better than that! Makes me feel better too, because if he's around protecting her, well, we're standing right next to her and I'm confident he'll step in to help us as well if the situation arose. Don't know if it works like that, but hey, I'll go with it anyway!

My good friend, orb researcher, and spirit rescue specialist Reverend Neal Farley upon hearing this said: *"That is wonderful and should give you and her solace in his presence."*

Here at *Castello Gallo*, believe it or not, I have personal experience with this approach that I could probably write a shorter book on. The best home protection is to have a cat. Yes, apparently ghosts don't like cats. I heard it may have something to do with their energy (auras). Others say that, like dogs, cats can clearly see ghosts and can actually frighten them away, even claw them! In any case, it works so well that I currently have three cats. Two indoors (Precious and Pookie) and one outdoors (Mr. Morris).

Having your house blessed by a priest is also a great idea. Yeah I know, it's the Catholic thing again.

Paranormal investigators versus ghost hunters

I have been asked on numerous occasions whether or not paranormal investigators and ghost hunters are the same thing? The answer is actually no, they are not. I believe there is a quantitative difference between the two which is this; paranormal investigators will take a piece of evidence and do everything they can to debunk it. If it survives the merciless onslaught of rationality, it makes the cut and becomes valid evidence. From their perspective it's the right thing to do.

On the other hand, ghost hunters will take the same piece of evidence and figure out reasons why it may be genuine. They will look at it in the context of the entire investigation to see if it corroborates with subsequent pieces of evidence (you will hear me talk about this perspective a lot) If it all makes sense, it makes the cut and becomes valid evidence. And from their perspective it is the right thing to do as well.

Both paranormal types are ultimately after the same thing, proof of the afterlife. But they have vastly different styles and ways of looking at things. One trip to a paranormal forum on social media will show you how strongly each camp feels about the way they look at the supernatural. Discussions often devolve into arguments very quickly.

I choose to follow the path of the ghost hunter simply because I see tons of potential evidence thrown into the wastebasket by paranormal investigators everyday. Some of this evidence is very compelling, but because there is even the *slightest chance* that it could be explained by conventional means; it is thrown out without ever taking into consideration the situation or circumstances surrounding how the evidence was captured.

I like to take one piece of evidence and fit it into the puzzle of the entire investigation if for no other reason than supporting evidence. So much should be taken into the context of each unique circumstance. For instance, I would never take an *Ovilus or ghost-box* session as sole evidence. But if I get a relevant word, or series of words, followed by high EMF, temperature fluctuations, and orbs all at the same time, my intuitive paranormal radar goes into alarm mode. And if it happens in an area known to have hauntings and paranormal activity, to me that is *Defcon 5* level compelling. These are often called *evidence strings* and the more strings you have, the closer you come to scientific proof.

By the way, as I am writing this, I feel that I should apologize if some of these terms seem Greek to readers who may be new to ghost hunting. Yes, we do indeed have our own lingo, terms, and acronyms, especially for equipment. In the investigations that follow I will clarify where I can.

You will also notice that I have included some shots from the investigations we will be discussing along with the episode title for each. So if you read something that intrigues you, we encourage you to visit our current web-series channel. Watch that episode and make your own critical judgement. We have had paranormal enthusiasts from all over the world catch EVP and other strange anomaly in our own episodes that we missed. Maybe you can as well!

A few words on skeptics

When you break it all down to it's lowest common denominator, a skeptic is basically *someone who attempts to attribute physical laws to non-physical entities.* Which from the outset is quite problematic when studying a *supernatural* world. After all, let's look at the actual

35

definition of the word <u>paranormal</u>: *An event or phenomena such as telekinesis or clairvoyance that is beyond the scope of normal scientific understanding.*

Skeptics come in many forms, and I spend a lot of time explaining their psyche only because I deal with them so frequently. For the reader who already believes in ghosts, or even shows this book to a skeptic, prepare yourself. You are probably going to get verbal backlash of some kind due to the various defense mechanisms they employ.

I have many good friends who are paranormal skeptics while being paranormal investigators themselves. They are great people and I often consider their opinions. I just disagree with the way they look at things for the most part. Some will tell you that being a skeptic doesn't mean you are a so-called *unbeliever*, and while that may be true, the term skeptic has become synonymous with the latter. Therefore, in order to keep things straight for the purposes of this book, I will reference the term skeptic as a blanket statement that can actually be used for both camps. The unbeliever, as well as the staunch, science minded paranormal investigator.

Skeptics as a whole have *created* debunks for virtually every form of paranormal experience. Yet, they cannot recreate the vast majority of it, despite what they say. If you get a *crystal clear* spirit image on film they will probably call it *Pareidolia* or *Matrixing*. Terms birthed in psychology that paranormal skeptics have taken to a whole new level. Same with *Electronic Voice Phenomena (EVP)* recordings. Regardless of how clear an EVP may sound, certain skeptics will still tell you that it is a figment of your imagination.

If you get respectable EMF readings in a remote cemetery or structure where there are no power lines or electricity sources whatsoever, they will suggest that it is coming from the earth itself in the form of *Geo-Location Energy*. Even though it's very rare for this type of EMF to emit energy strong enough to give substantial readings on a state-of-the-art Tri-Field EMF detector.

I even had one staunch skeptic tell me that my readings were due to sunspots! But, these same science/paranormal buffs will read about a faint repeating signal through a radio telescope from the far reaches of space and claim with certainty that it's caused by aliens. Even recently, there have been articles circulating around the internet explaining how "scientists" are attempting to open portals to alternate dimensions. Yup, this is solid science, but the existence of ghosts with it's various forms of evidence spanning the entire history of human civilization is just a mere flight of fancy. OK, Mr./Ms. Skeptic, keep telling yourself that.

The irony is incredible. But at least some still claim to be open minded and that's a good start. In other words, a few *aren't flat-out unbelievers*. But we deal with that type of personality all too frequently as well.

Although evidence captured through electronic means is valid. It is rarely repeatable. And that is what most skeptics will point to every time. My counter to that has always been the idea that we are dealing with entities who were once living, breathing people. That being the case, it's unlikely we will ever get repeatable evidence. They aren't trained monkeys here to entertain us. And we still don't know the process with which they manifest or communicate.

It may be quite difficult for ghosts to contact the living. Perhaps it's all dependent on location; or that environmental circumstances have to be just right. We just don't know at this juncture. *You cannot put a ghost in a bottle*. Therefore, we need to work with what we have.

Also, with the exception of the photographic, video, and electronic evidence, a great deal of paranormal evidence is anecdotal. And the more traditional science minded skeptics have a problem with that. Personal testimony is a grey area for skeptics. Those who saw, felt, or had a profound paranormal experience in any number of ways have always been our biggest advocates. The ironic thing where skeptics are concerned, is that personal testimony probably accounts for more *conversions* from skeptic to supernatural believer than any physical evidence ever could. I also like to remind them that *eyewitness testimony* is sometimes enough to convict in a court of law. My view is that anecdotal evidence is called *evidence* for a reason, and should always be considered.

So when someone pretends to be the smartest person in the room, always remember this argument stopper, which you have full permission to quote me on,

"There is a fine line between the scientific method, and blind skepticism."
  -Bobby J. Gallo

I have experienced all to frequently the *rationalist* who has their Rolodex of paranormal debunks ready for any occasion. No matter what you show them, they flip to a standard debunk. And usually, they will be as condescending as possible when they proudly tell you what their little index card says. The funny thing about paranormal "debunks" is that they are almost always based on a *probable cause* (ie. that orb is probably dust). So while it's rare that anomalies are 100% provable to be genuine paranormal activity, the reverse is also true in many cases. That is why I like to see if the debunk can be debunked itself so to speak. Gives you a more rounded perspective and doesn't pigeonhole you into one mode of thinking.

I already know that while many will find our evidence to be worthwhile and compelling, there are others out there in the vast reaches of "paranormal social media land" who will not be quite as impressed. As I gaze into my crystal ball (and I actually have one), I see mixed book reviews… And to be honest, I have absolutely no problem with that. Like I say repeatedly, *"there are no experts"* including us. Someday when we finally stumble upon, or are allowed to learn the truth, we can put these endless debates to rest. Until then, this is what we have, like it or not.

Phasmophobia

Phasmophobia is the fear of ghosts. The word originates from Greek word 'phasmos' which means 'supernatural being/phantom' and phobos which means 'deep dread or fear'. Another term for this condition is *Spectrophobia*, which originates from 'specters' or 'reflection'

I have had some skeptics come right out and tell me that the reason they don't believe is because *they don't want to believe.* Some have even expressed terror at the mere thought of an afterlife. Some would prefer oblivion to the notion of becoming a disembodied spirit. When these people are encountered, no amount of evidence will ever make them consider the possibility that ghosts exist. However, one cannot help but wonder if secretly they strongly believe in the supernatural to begin with, or they wouldn't be so terrified of ghosts in the first place.

This may be why the more militant skeptics will troll paranormal boards in an effort to knock down as much valid evidence as possible. Why they don't just avoid the subject altogether is another matter. But it does speak to their need for everyone to think like they do.

What exactly is pareidolia and matrixing?

This is the scientific term for how the human brain processes images in things like clouds in the sky or the Rorschach inkblot test. As I mentioned earlier, it's a very popular debunk with skeptics and they will use it with abandon. But it never bothers me, because often times, it's too automatic a response. Most will use it before they even consider the evidence at hand. So whenever this supposed debunk is presented to me, my retort is always, *"At what point does pareidolia become obvious recognition?"* I am usually greeted by stunned silence after this sinks in.

I firmly believe that spirits can manipulate matter in order to manifest so that we can see them (mists, orbs, etc.). In fact, when you think about it, that is how they *have to* operate. By definition, *a non-physical entity would have to manipulate physical properties in order to be seen by physical humans,* so who is to say how they perform that task at any given time? My two good friends, Hugh Fairman through water vapor experimentation, and Reverend Neal Farley using advanced orb photography, have been studying this paranormal image phenomenon for years with impressive results.

However, sometimes, things just fall into place that merely *look like* signs from beyond, and it's important to know the difference, but how do we do that?

The answer is to use common sense and intuition. Think of the situation, location, or timing of the image. But most importantly, it's clarity. Yes, I know this is basic, but it's important.

When deciphering a possibly paranormal image, these factors should be taken into consideration:

- Are there features that make this an undeniable human or animal image?
- Are there *tell-tale* similarities to the ghost when he/she was living?
- Is there a clear-cut reason for this image? Was it a sign of sorts?
- Was it taken during an investigation at a haunted or religious location?
- Was there a paranormal communication like a seance going on at the time?

These are just a few examples, but it's important to consider them, because the sad fact for many hard-core *believers* is that not everything will be paranormal. The average person will be able to see a face in almost anything given enough time and effort. Which is evidenced by the thousands of so-called paranormal pictures on social media where people, out of sheer necessity, with have to circle an area of a photo which you have to study for hours just to see what they are talking about. These photos discredit what we do and I truly wish people would think more before posting these online. Same goes for garbled and unintelligible EVP (we have thrown hundreds of those out from our own investigations). It only gives the die-hard skeptics and unbelievers fuel to mercilessly bash what we do.

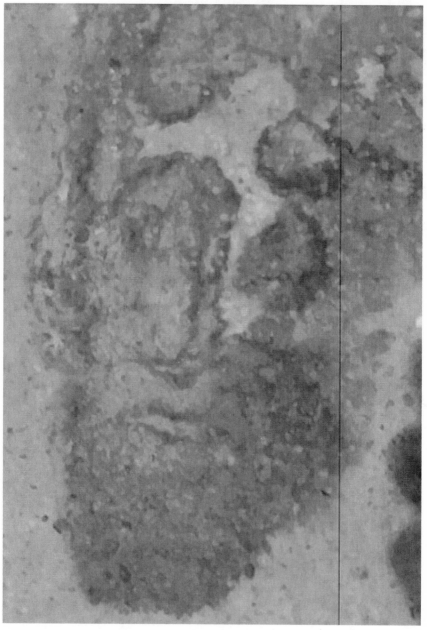

An example of <u>pareidolia</u>. Image of Abe Lincoln after his encounter with John Wilkes Booth, on the dungeon floor of Castello Gallo, after a towel soaked with heating oil accidentally mixed with water, staining the concrete... Unfortunately this was not caused by a ghost... I think.

3

Ghost Hunting Terms & Tech

I already know from friends and fans on our social media pages who expressed interest in the writing of this book, that a good majority know little or nothing about ghost hunting and paranormal investigation other than what they see in our videos. And let's face it, if you see us interacting with our ITC equipment, the average person is probably not going to understand what is going on. To that end, I felt this chapter to be necessary. The seasoned pro investigators reading this will get some benefits and insights out of the following. But it is intended mostly for those who are venturing into these dark woods for the first time.

What are the tools and tech that make ghost hunting work? What are a few of the terms and equipment used? That is what we will be discussing in this chapter. This is a primer of sorts and will prepare the reader for the verbiage, and technical terms that will be used in the explanations of the investigations (episodes) to follow, but first...

The three main areas of afterlife research

Ghost hunting/paranormal investigative: Since this is a book on ghost hunting, we will pretty much stick with this genre. It's also the reason I won't spend too much time on it here. This is the practice of gathering evidence of the afterlife primarily through cutting edge electronic techniques such as ITC (Instrumental Transcommunication), digital and emulsion photography, digital and analog audio, as well as digital video. Then mixing it all up with classic divination practices like dowsing.

Mediumship and clairvoyance: Gathering evidence through those gifted with the ability to psychically bridge the gap between here and the hereafter. The key "here" is to differentiate between the genuine article (and I firmly believe these people exist), the fraud who is only out there for fame and money, and those who confuse psychic with psychosis through no fault of their own.

Being a magician, I am more than familiar with how one can fool the masses into thinking they are a genuine mentalist or medium. I actually have books in my extensive library which give instruction on how to do this. Unfortunately, one is actually authored by a "medium" who's client base are Hollywood celebrities. Obviously, it's a guide to fraudulent mediumship and I think it's disgraceful. We have a hard enough time getting the scientific community to take us seriously as it is without these charlatans giving us a bad name.

This is a very rare device (complete with instructions) used by fraudulent mediums to produce rapping sounds during a seance. It is tied around the mid-section very tightly... Then by carefully using the solar-plexus muscles, the noises can be produced on command to answer questions posed by unsuspecting sitters. I sold it to a collector of such spooky artifacts.

NDE afterlife research, parapsychology, and metaphysics: Probably the most promising avenue when it comes to proving consciousness survival. And arguably even more scientific than what we do as ghost hunters and paranormal investigators. Because the bulk of these studies are being carried out by doctors and scientists themselves. The evidence they are compiling is astounding, and their credentials are above reproach.

For example, *Near Death Experience* (NDE) research which started in the 1970's and is still being complied today, has shown through literally thousands of known cases, that those who were clinically dead, were still conscious in some form that the scientific community still does not understand, defying the teachings of conventional medicine. Those who have experienced an NDE, more times than not, have also had experiences that are in perfect synchronicity with others who have undergone the same process of dying and then returning to the living.

NDE falls under the umbrella of *parapsychology* which is an all encompassing scientific field that also includes telepathy, precognition, clairvoyance, psychokinesis, synchronicity, reincarnation, and apparitional experiences (ghosts).

While most people stick with one field, I study all four. There is much to be gained from each. And from what I have learned, incredible evidential similarities between them. Which I believe is a great example of *cross validation*.

Bare bones ghost hunting kit

All beginning ghost hunters need a starting point. This is where we began and it may help to serve as a launching pad for those interested in ghost hunting after reading this book.

Before daring our first paranormal outing, we went in search of equipment. I knew we needed at least several things in order for us to go ghost hunting. Again, this list is a starting point only. Today, we have an extensive line of equipment for all phases of supernatural investigation. Though it is vitally important to point out that the very best ghost hunting tools are your own senses and intuition.

1.SONY DCR-DVD92 NTSC Video Camera With Night Vision.
If we were going to do this, I wanted everything captured on digital disk. I never new at the time that the Sony Handycam I had purchased a year prior, and had been using for family vacations actually had infrared night vision called *NightShot,* which is basically the same technology used on the ghost hunting television shows. Talk about freaking out when I found that out!

I have to say that I love this camera for paranormal work. I even went back to it after purchasing a newer digital model that kept files on a small memory card. The Sony takes television quality video that is superior in many ways to that of more current models. And keeps them permanently on a physical disk for back-up. Something that current cameras do not do. Though they don't make this model anymore, as of this writing there seem to be a large amount of them on eBay for pretty reasonable prices. Grab one if you want a truly great ghost hunting video camera. Disks for them are still readily available.

2.Bell+Howell S7 Slim Compact Digital Camera With Night Vision: I purchased a night vision still camera which I use to this day. Unfortunately they are no longer made and very hard to find.

3.Electromagnetic Field (EMF) Detector: I happened upon the one piece of equipment that we have used more than any other. It's also the one that has caused the most controversy amongst the more scientifically minded paranormal skeptics, *The Ghost Meter Pro.* A modified EMF detector which incorporates a *seance mode* to communicate with energies by pinging the needle when you ask *yes or no* questions. We'll discuss this piece of equipment, the controversy surrounding it, and our experience using it after the recap of our very first encounter as a family ghost hunting team.

4.RCA Digital Voice Recorder: I ordered a very basic hand held RCA digital recorder from Amazon. Nothing fancy, but it's a real workhorse that has captured great evidence. Even though later in our careers we actually started receiving donations from paranormal fans and admirers in the way of equipment, some very expensive digital ZOOM recorders included. Our small hand held RCA recorder remains our *go-to*. My opinion is that if it works well, why switch?

5.Black+Decker Infrared Temperature Gun: It was late Dr. Harry Stafford, the world famous *Indiana Jones of paranormal investigators*, who taught us the proper methods of using temperature guns to capture paranormal evidence. We use a standard Black+Decker version that is normally sold to detect energy leaks within a home. The nice thing about this particular thermal gun is that it visually shows you exactly where the temperature changes happen by shining a light that changes color when the fluctuation occurs. Great for video evidence, and also for the fact that you can keep your eyes on the activity location and not constantly on the digital screen of the unit. These are still available as of the writing of this book and are highly recommended.

Further ghost hunting gear

There is so much currently available in the marketplace that it would be nearly impossible to cover it all. So I will only list the other pieces of gear that we presently use. Many of them will be explained in detail in the investigations to follow.

1. P-SB7 Spirit Box
2. Full spectrum camera

3. Laser Grid with mini tripod
4. Static-Pod by Professional Measurement
5. Electromagnetic frequency (EMF) pump
6. Motion detectors
7. Walkie Talkies
8. Spirit Touch by Gotcha Ghost
9. Audio puck by Altec Lansing
10. Dowsing rods
11. Clear quartz crystal pendulum
12. Standard pocket compass
13. EVP mic by Digital Dowsing
14. Tri-Field EMF detector
15. K2 EMF detector
16. ZOOM stereo digital recorder
17. External IR "Phantom" lights
18. Camera shoulder harness
19. Go Pro camera with chest mount
20. Video sunglasses
21. Multi beam flashlight
22. Mag light with red lens
23. Multi color light-sticks
24. Various paranormal test apps
25. Insect repellent (seriously)

This was our basic gear kit a very short time after we began investigating. Today we have much more. Notice the pendulum on the tripod. This was my first home-made ghost detector based upon theories I learned as a professional magician. Also the infamous and controversial "Ghost Meter Pro" seen on the extreme right hand side of the photo.

EMF and ghosts

You are probably wondering by now why we use EMF detectors to detect ghosts? Aren't these precision instruments supposed to be used to detect leaks in a microwave or test the insulation of power lines in your home? Yes, they are, but it's also theorized that ghosts, when they enter the earthly plane either do so though *electromagnetic energy*

50

fields or are electromagnetic in nature themselves. Or perhaps it's the type of energy they use to manifest themselves under certain conditions.

Although very small and difficult to measure, humans have an electromagnetic field around them which dissipates after death. Anytime there is an electric current, a magnetic field is produced and in the process of our bodies operation, there are many electric currents and voltages produced. But since *energy can neither be created nor destroyed*, the question has always remained, what happens to this electromagnetic energy when we die? Well, the answer may be right in front of us pinging the needle on our EMF detectors.

Many psychics claim that they can see this energy field which some call the *aura*. The more religious have referred to it as the *halo*. New age advocates will say there are various colors and aspects to it known as the *Chakras*. Is there a possible connection? Many Parapsychologists thinks so, and so do I.

So all of those old scary stories and movies about ghosts appearing during thunderstorms may have a basis in fact after all. Paranormal researchers (including us) even charge areas with EMF or Ionization energy prior to investigations in the hopes that spirits can feed off of said energy in order to help them manifest. To further prove this point, battery drain is one of the most common experiences of the ghost hunter. It's suspected that ghosts will feed off of this energy as well, and it has happened to us *countless* times. To validate this theory, we have observed that most every time it has happened in a given area, we have had paranormal activity in that same location.

It's also theorized that ghosts may actually feed off of *our own* energy fields if they have nothing else to tap. This may be the reason that many ghost hunters feel drained during or after an investigation (sometimes referred to as *paranormal hangover*). Hey, we're the ones asking them to manifest, they are just obliging us right?

Our specially designed Tri-Field EMF detector; often considered the absolute best unit of it's kind for paranormal investigation as it can filter out man-made EMF in order to detect only organic frequencies. Here it is in action, attempting to detect possible paranormal energy at Gettysburg Battlefield. Notice the photo was shot in Infrared. This was an attempt to capture photographic evidence should an entity approach the equipment as per our request.

EVP: Electronic Voice Phenomenon

EVP is the act of recording an investigation with a digital recorder in the hopes of capturing a ghost actually speaking. The theory is that ghosts speak on a frequency human ears cannot hear, but one that digital recorders can. Dogs for example can hear a dog whistle, but we cannot, same with ghosts. Which would explain the theories why pets seem to hear spirits and while humans just stare at them in puzzlement.

Nicky G. conducting a "real-time" EVP session while shooting at Gettysburg Battlefield in an attempt at ethereal communication. - Ghosts & Girls In Gettysburg

AVP: Audible Voice Phenomenon

Pretty much the same as an EVP except for the fact that you can actually hear this phenomenon with your own ears and thus do not need electronic assistance. However, having a recorder or video camera running allows you to obtain *substantiated evidence* where an AVP on it's own becomes merely *anecdotal evidence.*

Other types of sound waves such as animal sounds, unexplained creaking noises, ethereal footsteps, knocking sounds, etc. also fall under the umbrella term AVP.

Cold spots

Cold spots are areas which undergo a sudden decrease in ambient temperature for no apparent reason. This phenomenon has been closely tied to paranormal activity since ancient times. Why this happens is anyone's guess. Perhaps it has something to do with a ghosts need to absorb energy. In this case heat, from it's surroundings before possible manifestation. Other theories suggest that ghosts, consisting of energy themselves may affect the environment through spiritual portals or vortexes which may be of differing temperatures than those of normal surroundings.

Since we are on this subject, it bears repeating that using a temperature gun to detect possible paranormal activity was one of the very first ghost hunting techniques taught to us by the late Dr. Harry Stafford. Even some of the most advanced paranormal equipment designed today such as the *Mel-Meter* contain features that measure ambient temperature. For these reasons, the temperature gun remains one of the primary tools in the ghost hunters arsenal.

Paranormal photography

There are paranormal investigators and ghost hunters who do nothing but take video and photographs during an investigation. "Orb hunters" are especially prone to this singular method of evidence collection. Taking photos and videos are also very low impact ways to ghost hunt. Since there seems to be very little contact with entities and a respectable distance is maintained between the ghost and the observer. Unless of course, you start *asking* them to appear. When you do that, you are technically conducting a *seance*.

It must be stressed that some cameras seem to work better than others when it comes to photographing paranormal anomalies. There are literally entire forums on social media devoted to this topic, as well as entire books written on the subject. So it's good to test different cameras if you have the means to see what units are capable of capturing evidence and which ones do not. The most important thing to remember is that having a camera is critical to your investigation. Even if it's just the camera on your cell phone.

"Without documentation, all you will ever have is a good ghost story."
  -Bobby J. Gallo

Lately, I have have heard of camera companies applying special coatings to the lens of newer camera models in order to filter out orbs which is something I was afraid was going to happen sooner or later. I am of the belief that paranormal orbs reside in a certain spectrum of light. And if you find a way to filter that spectrum out, this aspect of paranormal science may become extinct and our understanding of these anomalies will be compromised. So in your search for a camera with which to investigate, perhaps it may be advantageous to find an older model on eBay or other similar outlet.

ITC: Instrumental Transcommunication

The Ghost Meter Pro, The Ghost Speaker app, and ghost box apps such as the SV1 SpiritVox, are known as ITC or Instrumental Transcommunication devices. This method of communication with the spirit world using the advanced electronics of the day isn't some made up flight of fancy. Beginning around the turn of the 20th century through today, ITC was pioneered by many brilliant men of science and technology. Such men as Waldemar Bogoras, Roberto Landell, Thomas Alva Edison (yes, that one!), Oscar d'Argonell, Attila von Szalay, Friedrich Juergenson, Franz Seidel, Dr. Konstantin Raudive, Marcello Bacci, Frank Sumption, Gary Galka, and many others.

For example, Gary Galka owns a company which designs and manufactures cutting edge electronic measuring devices. But when family tragedy struck, he set out to find a way to contact *the other side.* As a result, he has created some of the most cutting edge paranormal investigation equipment in the world such as the famous *P-SB7 Spirit Box* and the *Mel-Meter.* We currently use two of his devices. One of which we will be talking about later in the book.

Another pioneer in this field is Bill Chapell of Digital Dowsing. His creations have been seen on the hit TV series *Ghost Adventures.* The world owes these gentlemen and others like Daniel Roberge creator of the *Echovox* and *SV1 SpiritVox* a great debt of gratitude for giving us the tools needed to peek through the veil between this plane of existence and the next.

How do all of these electronic marvels work? Many ghost hunters and paranormal researchers surmise that a spirit's ability to communicate through electronic means despite it's age (even if the ghost is hundreds of years old), may be due to *Universal Intelligence or Morphic Field* theories. The spirits *just know*. And evidence of this has been shown over and over again by these devices spitting out words, phrases, and other data that are just too relevant and thematic in nature to dismiss.

An opposing viewpoint

There is an article currently circulating around the internet stating that one of the pioneers in ITC research is an unbeliever on the subject of ghosts and spirits. Therefore, skeptics will gleefully point to this story to use as "proof" that all of this technology is BS in order to capitalize on the current paranormal phenomenon and wishful thinking of those who want to believe in an afterlife.

But consider this, the designers of the digital camera inadvertently created a device that can see spectrum of light that we cannot (I talk more about this in chapter #6). Likewise, the developers of the digital recorder never in their wildest dreams knew it could capture the whispers of spirit. And last but not least, the EMF detector was never designed to detect or communicate with paranormal energies, *but here we are.*

It's also important to mention that history is full of examples where the intention was to invent something for one stated purpose and inadvertently stumble upon another. So it's no surprise that those who set out to develop an ITC device actually achieve it despite a belief system to the contrary. Moreover, who's to say that the intent of the end user doesn't influence how these technological marvels perform? After all, isn't all of this technology merely dowsing with batteries? Plus, as we have already discussed, theoretically it's possible for the entity itself to influence many of these devices.

Finally, perhaps these developers achieved these inspired creations by tapping unknowingly into *Universal Intelligence* or the *Morphic Field* themselves? Hey, it's a stretch I know, but it's food for thought.

If the above terms seem a bit confusing, no worries, they will be discussed in greater detail in Chapter #5 when we experience our very first ITC communication using…

The Ghost Meter Pro (GMP)

You are going to see a lot of this particular piece of equipment. Especially in the early investigations, so just a few words on it. I purchased two of them and it's good that I did since they are nearly impossible to find now. As is the case with nearly all pieces of equipment exclusively designed for paranormal field use. A set number are made, sold, and then you never see them again.

What makes the GMP unique is that it isn't just a garden variety EMF detector such as the one Grant Wilson used extensively on the hit paranormal TV show *Ghost Hunters* (he used a K2). The GMP has a mode on it that can be triggered to begin a dialogue with a ghost if the conditions are right. Now I know how far fetched that sounds, and I thought so too at first. So I contacted the manufacturer of the unit via email and flat-out asked if this was genuine or for entertainment purposes only.

The answer was fast and clear. The developers unapologetically vouched for it's authenticity. High EMF levels trigger the communication mode then act accordingly with subtle EMF spikes during the *seance mode*. Now this can also happen in a high EMF atmosphere without a ghost present as well. There have even been YouTube videos where skeptics have attempted to debunk this unit by turning it on and letting it run until it triggers communication mode and that is actually normal. If on long enough it will trigger by default because the *Ghost Meter Pro* is searching for EMF which it eventually finds. Especially in a video studio! So it's important to sweep the area in regular EMF detection mode first. Once man made EMF can be ruled out for the most part, the GMP becomes a more credible tool.

This unit was also featured during an investigation on *The National Geographic Channel (Nat Geo)* And has been used by such notable and respected paranormal researchers as Fiona Broome.

The Ghost Speaker by Krugism Development LLC

First of all, this is not a paid endorsement. I am including the following explanation simply because the *Ghost Speaker* is the best paranormal phone app we have ever used. I have no idea what magic Scott Krug used to develop this incredible software program but take my advice and try it, you won't be disappointed.

This phone app appears to work in a fashion similar to the famous *Ovilus* device seen on television shows such as *Ghost Adventures &* *Paranormal State*. The GS contains 2,854 random names and words in a *dictionary file*. I contacted Scott Krug, the developer of the Ghost Speaker to relate some of the incredible experiences we have had with his creation. He explained it to me this way in his own words,

"The app uses the EMF, orientation, and the light sensor to generate which record to read from the dictionary.... But, it's crazy the words that come up referencing something relevant, or several words together that make sense.... I've heard quite a few stories about the same thing.... I programmed it, and I have no idea why it works so good."

The widely-held theory amongst ghost hunters and paranormal researchers is that an entity can use the phone's sensors in apps like the Ghost Speaker to pick out certain words from the dictionary in order to communicate. This technique has delivered incredible results for many investigators including us. And has an advantage over traditional EVP in the sense that evidence cannot be tainted by sound contamination (background sounds that can be misconstrued as EVP). Also, unlike a traditional ghost box such as the P-SB7, the communication is crystal clear and not subject to possible misinterpretation.

A few words on cell phone ghost hunting apps

We have tried literally dozens of apps, we even started using a phone-app called the *Ghost-O-Meter* which I believe is no longer available. In many episodes you will also see us using apps such as *Phantom Radar, Ghost Radar, SV-1 SpiritVox, Spirit Voice, The Ghost Speaker,* among others.

We've tested so many, some were genuine and some were not. The ones listed above made the cut. It's important to note that the developers of these cell phone apps do so for different reasons. Some are purely for entertainment purposes only and DO NOT assist in genuine paranormal investigation. In fact, some actually FAKE evidence and should be shunned at all costs unless your goal is simply to freak people out at the next party.

Others are developed by those who are actual paranormal investigators themselves such as my good friend and colleague Daniel Roberge of Bigbeard Studios. He creates paranormal apps with the intent gathering actual evidence. His *Echovox* is used all over the world by thousands of experienced investigators. It's critical that you know what you are using and who developed it.

It's also important to realize that the modern cell phone is a marvel of electronic genius. The sensors in the phone such as the magnetometer (critical for paranormal apps) and the accelerometer can be used to detect and interpret electromagnetic energies as well as motion. Some apps also use your phone mic for EVP purposes, as well as create a sonar effect that can detect the same frequencies that ghosts use to deliver EVP. We can tell what frequencies these are when we analyze EVP in a robust audio editing suite such as *Audacity*.

We have had great success with these apps when used as *supporting evidence*. In other words, they are rarely evidence in and of themselves. We like to use the radar or sonar apps as *leads* if you will. Once we get the location of a signal, we head in that direction with the rest of our equipment. It may be a spirit, or again, it may be random EMF energy. We would need more in order to make a determination. The Ghost Speaker app however is phenomenal on it's own. It has captured every bit as much relevant communication as it's more expensive counterpart, the *Ovilus* which is used by the big TV para-celebs and currently costs hundreds of dollars in it's current version.

IMPORTANT: Without a magnetometer in your phone, most of these apps default to simulation mode and you will be left with what is basically a toy.

Dowsing rods, Ouija boards, and pendulums

Since the Victorian spiritualist era, the primary way to communicate with ghosts has always been the classic seance. This was done in large part with the infamous Ouija board. There is a lot of controversy surrounding this type of equipment due to the fear that it may contact entities in the "other" category. While it's true that the *ideomotor effect* or *subconscious muscle movement* moves the planchette; many feel, myself included, that it's spirit using the people seated at the table as a *conduit* if you will. If this is true, and I think it is, then it may pose certain risks. Dowsing rods and pendulums (the latter of which I am rather good at using btw) work the same way. This is why in the videos you would sometimes see Renee completely exhausted after using the rods. They definitely seem to cause a drain on her personal energy.

Also the materials that these instruments are made of have a dramatic influence on how effectively they will work in the field. For instance, dowsing rods should be made of copper as this metal is a superb conductor of electromagnetic energy. Pendulums come in a myriad of crystal and other types of material. But in my experience, nothing beats clear quartz. Clear quartz enhances psychic abilities, aids concentration, and unlocks memory. Mine was even charged with *reiki life force* (or so I was told). Regardless, it is the best pendulum I have used to communicate with otherworldly energies.

As a final thought on this subject. When initiating contact with an entity, there is a distinction between using equipment such as an EMF detector vs. the conduit methods such as dowsing and the boards as far as risk is concerned. As I mentioned in Chapter #2. I think protection is important no matter what. But I think it is *critical* when contemplating the conduit methods.

4

Paranormal Pioneers

I t's important to note that my first paranormal investigation was conducted a full decade before the popular ghost hunting television shows and present day paranormal phenomenon. Back then, I really had nothing to go on as far as examples and role models were concerned.

At the risk of sounding self-aggrandizing, I was a pioneer in the field. I was completely winging it with my own ideas. The only guidance I had was from an outdated book by magician John Booth entitled *Psychic Paradoxes*. Little did I know that the methods I came up with and used in conducting this early investigation weren't all that different from what many investigators are using today, albeit the equipment and verbiage have changed, so I must have been doing something right.

In this case, I am going to reprint with permission, a synopsis of this investigation from the original ICOM Paranormal Wordpress blog written seven years ago.

Investigating The Haunted Palace Theater – Netcong NJ

Posted in Ghost Hunts on January 12, 2012 by ICOM Paranormal

The Palace Theater was built in 1919 by my Great Uncle John Gallo. It started as a silent movie and vaudeville house, then moved on to talkies, other community events, and entertainment.

The Historic Palace Theater during it's hay day

In 1934 it was leased by a prominent Newark theater operator and major renovation began with fabric wall coverings and ceiling drapes. In 1938, there was a marquee added and the Colonial Revival facade was covered by Art Deco style.

The Palace Theater was the *try out* theater for many famous actors before hitting Broadway. Live theater performers such as George Burns and Gracie Allen, Milton Berle, and Bud Abbott, all toured the country with their vaudeville acts. Many stopping in at the Palace

Theater in Netcong. Newly released popular movies also appeared over the next two decades.

In the mid-1940's the commercial storefronts in it's facade were removed and the Palace Theater continued as a movie house into the 1960's. Then competition took hold from television and eventually from multiplexes. It was converted into a warehouse in 1981 until 1994. This is the time period when much of the alleged paranormal activity took place. It was also the time when we performed our first ghost hunt.

Since then it was purchased in May 1995 by *The Growing Stage Children's Theater of New Jersey* and is now a performing arts center. It survived long enough to make it onto the *National Register of Historic Places* which is fortunate as rumors of it being torn down over the decades had me more than fearful of it's ultimate fate.

It was during the years just prior to it's renaissance, when the theater was purchased by a moving company and no longer showing movies when mysterious phenomena began to occur. The owner of the theater allegedly had items as large as small appliances thrown at him, hearing disembodied voices, and the actual self-playing of a haunted piano on the top floor. Psychics were then brought in who apparently confirmed that the theater was being haunted by not one, but two ghosts by the names of *Malcolm and Jenny* who were said to haunt not only the theater at large, but particularly the old piano on the very top floor above the balcony. Not much is known about these two spirits other than the information passed through mediums that they were somehow connected with the theater's past. And now they were restless because the structure was no longer a showplace.

I heard a great deal of this story from various sources including a man who was a good friend of mine at the time by the name of Lou Batson.

Lou was an elderly gentleman who flew biplanes before WWII, and worked as a projectionist at the theater for many years. We would talk at length for hours about the history of the theater and it's inhabitants. I also learned things about my Great Uncles and Grandfather that I never would have otherwise known if it were not for Lou. For this I will be eternally grateful to him. This history was important because of the fact that my since my Great Uncles built the Palace, there may be a clue somewhere in that information that could solve the riddle of Malcolm and Jenny.

Yes, the family connection; that coupled with my innate appreciation of the supernatural filled me with incredible excitement and determination to find out what was going on for myself. So I paid a visit to the theater during daylight hours and spoke to the owner. He confirmed everything I was told and gave me permission to come back any evening I liked to investigate. He told me that the night watchman would be there and would be instructed to let me and my team in, *but that he himself wouldn't go near the place at night!* He was visibly shaken when he spoke about the theater since he had first hand experience with poltergeist activity there and having had items like *bread toasters* literally thrown at him.

I assembled a team of interested friends to help me investigate. For understandable reasons, I didn't want to do it alone. The team consisted my myself, Mike Emma, Brian J. Orlowski, and Shawn Bates. We dubbed ourselves *THE PSY-GUYS*. Since at that time there was really no such thing as ghost hunting as we know it today, we brought the only things we thought we needed. A few flashlights, a mini-tape recorder, a video camera, a still 35mm camera, a candle, and a home-made pendulum which was nothing more than an old key on a piece of string.

Ghost Hunting at the Historic Palace Theatre
Netcong New Jersey

(c) 2012 International Conservatory of Magic

Before the Para-Celebs and ghost hunting television shows of today... THE PSY-GUYS... The original paranormal investigators, ghost hunters, or whatever we were.

When we got there we were greeted by the night watchman named Harry. He echoed almost verbatim what the owner had said and told us about all sorts of activity in the theater. Additionally, he said that we were on our own in the investigation as he never sets foot outside of the office, or even into the lobby after the sun went down! Night watchman indeed...

Sufficiently freaked out, we first searched the main body of the theater which was packed with junk as it was a moving and storage facility at the time (again, this was the main reason the ghosts were said to haunt the place). Looking up we could still see the great velvet drapes that flanked the ceiling and the hammered tin tiles. Luxuries from a bygone era. Other than creaks and echoes from our footsteps, this part of our investigation did not turn up much of anything, but it sure was creepy! Even when Mike Emma from our team called out to Malcolm and Jenny to make themselves known to us there was no response.

We then went up to the balcony where the old projection booth was. Here was one of the spots where activity was said to have taken place (where things were thrown from). On the floor were littered relics of it's theater past. Check out this actual photo of a poster advertising the newest movie of the time, Shenandoah with James Stuart! WOW! A few people (who weren't there) have told me after seeing this photo that I should have taken this piece of history since it was probably trashed eventually anyway. But I think that when you are ghost hunting, you must respect the property where you are. The last thing you need to be doing is stealing from already restless spirits!

Never take anything home from an investigation... Not even this vintage poster... That can be the surest way to have an unwanted, ethereal house-guest.

Now it was time to go to the top floor above the balcony. We were all nervous as this was supposedly the most active part of the theater. The home of the haunted piano.

As we got to the top of the landing we noted that all of the windows to the top room were boarded up. Pigeons nested in the space between the old broken panes and the boards themselves. The room was long with a large WWII propeller adorning the far wall as this hall was used as a nightclub decades ago for USO shows.

As we were exploring with our flashlights as our sole source of illumination, we suddenly became aware of the smell of fresh cut flowers! I swung my flashlight to the left and in the corner of the room I saw it. A massive decaying piano with what appeared to be a vase of fresh flowers upon it! Strange, I thought to myself. Why would there be flowers here? Nevertheless, we examined the piano. All of the keys seemed frozen save for a few which Brian, one of our team members began lightly tapping. All of a sudden the birds in the windows became very agitated. The more Brian played the notes (which were not all that audible mind you) the more agitated the birds got. Once he stopped, so did the birds.

Haunted piano with possible manifestation

We snapped a few 35mm shots of the piano (pictured above) and then went down stairs. What is curious about the developed photo of the keyboard is that you will notice some kind of fabric or lace hanging down in front of the picture after the film was developed. None of the investigators ever remember seeing this when we were there. And

I certainly would have taken the picture from another angle to avoid it at the time. What is it and how did it get there? To this day we have no idea.

Once we got back down to the ground floor we took one more walk around the main area of the theater. It was then that a golf ball seemed to fly in our direction. *Was this the infamous poltergeist activity the theater was known for?* We immediately investigated in the area where the ball came from and found nothing. We did however, find the ball. Again, today there is no satisfactory explanation for this occurrence.

We then went back to Harry "the night watchman" to debrief him on what had happened. He didn't seem a bit surprised and was actually amazed that we didn't get far more activity given the recent history of the place. When I asked him about the flowers near the piano, he told us that they were requested by the spirits of Malcolm and Jenny through a psychic who was there before us at the request of a notable television documentary program (I was told it was NOVA but I have never been able to confirm this). He then laughed and asked about their appearance?

We all agreed that they looked like they were freshly picked. In fact, the entire room smelled like a funeral parlor full of flowers. He grew pale and fell silent. *"What's the matter?"* I asked. He replied: *"Those flowers were put up there months ago and no one has watered or seen to them since..."*

*Lou Batson has since passed on; however, Steve Fredericks of the current theater company (The Growing Stage Children's Theater of New Jersey) who now runs the establishment recently told me that they believe Lou himself is now haunting the place as well as Malcolm and Jenny. And they have valid reasons for thinking so. Folks, I couldn't make this stuff up if I tried. I may have to go and pay my old friend another visit for old time sake!

Investigating The Haunted Palace Theater - Early 1990's

Present day thoughts: We actually did several astounding follow-up investigations of this theater which will be discussed in later chapters. But this early investigation does go to show that we really didn't need fancy equipment to go ghost hunting at the time. Just a plan and nerves of steel.

5

Real Family-Real Life-Real Ghosts

Castello Gallo - A 1928 Italianate Brick Castle, complete with dungeon and hidden rooms... "Gallo Family Ghost Hunters" haunted home sweet home... Yes, we really do live here.

I t was 2007 and the decision was made to end my career as a full-time professional magician. By this time Renee and I had become parents of the two best kids anyone could possibly ask for. So being on the road as a magician was out of the question at this point. The responsibilities of being a father and the necessity of a full-time paycheck with benefits far outweighed the need to *live in the limelight*. Though, I still perform to this day on a semi-professional basis. When our ghostly adventures began, I was earning my living in sales. Plus, still maintaining the *International Conservatory of Magic Online* as yet another side-line.

At the time, we lived in Fort Mill South Carolina. The area was rich in southern charm and history. Dilapidated ruins of the old Jim and Tammy Baker religious theme park only blocks from our home. In retrospect, this area was far creepier than most of our investigations.

Renee and I had raised Nicolet (who took the name Nicky G. for the show) and Courtnee into brave young woman. They were two kids with polar opposite personalities who seem to compliment each other. Nicolet was ROTC at Nation Ford High and Courtnee was miss popularity in her elementary school.

We spent our nights watching television as most families do, and had just burned through every episode of *Dark Shadows on HULU*, when one show in particular caught our attention, *Ghost Adventures on The Travel Channel*. Those three guys fascinated the family, myself included. We also watched *Ghost Hunters, Most Haunted*, and several other paranormal shows. They seemed to be popping up everywhere, but the family favorite was clearly *Ghost Adventures*.

One night as we were watching our favorite ghost sleuthing trio, I turned to the kids and said, *"You know kids, daddy used to do that too."* The world literally stopped as they turned to me, wide eyed

First Contact

Those who have watched this rather low-key episode saw Nicky G, Courtnee, and myself (with Renee on camera) making contact with our very first entity. There was a lot of historical information that I had to learn in order to sound like I knew what I was talking about and that alone makes it worth watching to a small degree. And in a humorous vein, it's also the time I coined the phrase *ambient spirits*. Whatever that means.

Right off the bat I am going to say that this wasn't our most compelling investigation. But it was our first as a family and because of that it's significant. I had never used the *Ghost Meter Pro (GMP)* before, and refused to try it out before the actual investigation. In fact, it's been a policy of mine since the very beginning of our ghost hunting endeavors that *we never ghost hunt at home, ever!* That means we don't try out new gear that is designed for ethereal communication until the actual investigation. Why? Because there is always the risk of *stirring up* spiritual energy in the place where you sleep. More times than not, it's unwelcome, and can be difficult to get rid of once it appears. So take my advice, if you plan on ghost hunting, begin and end the investigation at the site. Also, as I said in the previous chapter, *do not bring anything home with you,* even something as simple as a cool looking rock from the cemetery. Objects have been know to carry ghostly attachments. If you have ever watched the television series *Haunted Collector* with John Zaffis (The Godfather of the paranormal) you will know exactly what I am referring to. So take heed.

Back to the episode. We installed with a fresh 9 volt battery, powered up the Ghost Meter Pro, approached the old structure, and began to do our sweep of the front porch. It was a few minutes of nothing. Personally, I didn't think we were going to get anything and I already started to wonder if this was all just a giant waste of time.

Then after a few more minutes the meter started to react which signaled that we detected some kind of EMF energy. Possibly even a spirit since there was no power to speak of around this small house. We switched the Ghost Meter Pro into dialogue mode not knowing what to expect and continued to clumsily walk around the porch and windows.

Then it happened, the Ghost Meter Pro triggered into communication mode. My heart was in my throat, was this really happening? Courtnee was right there beside me helping to interview our unseen guest. From the beginning she was utterly fearless. She knew this was a ghost and she simply didn't care. I think I was more nervous that she was. Using the few questions we had at the ready, we soon came to the conclusion that the entity was most likely that of Billy Graham's grandfather.

Now, by this time, the reader who is new to the paranormal may already be asking, *"How can we assume that the spirit was that of Mr. Graham senior?"* Great question!, and here is the answer…

The spirit communication in this circumstance works like this, at least in the ghost hunting sense. We ask the spirit to ping the needle on the Ghost Meter Pro, once means "yes," twice means "no." We then begin questioning the entity. Through a series of simple questions we attempt to unravel the mystery of who they are and why they are here, until the communication terminates.

So throughout this book, you will hear me refer to a *Ghost Meter Pro (or the abbreviation GMP)* communication or whatever piece of equipment we are using at the time. This is how every session is conducted. It's an exciting experience. One that can also be done with a regular EMF detector (albeit, not as effectively), dowsing rods, pendulums, Ouija boards (which I do not recommend BTW) etc.

It's also important to note that we were getting regular EMF spikes on the porch as well, indicating energy in an area where there should have been none at all, before we made contact which is always a paranormal alert!

The big takeaway from this groundbreaking investigation (for us anyway) was the looming question as to why this gentlemen was at his earthly home in the first place? If he was indeed the grandfather of one of the world's most famous evangelists, *"Why was he not in Heaven?"* Or if he was/is there, *"How does he travel back and forth to his homestead?"* *"Can he do it on a whim?"* *"Is he in both places at the same time?"* *"Was this spirit simply an impostor?"* *"Or can we just chalk all of this up to random EMF in the area pinging the needle in answer to our questions?"* The last question was sarcasm.

Here is another pertinent question the beginner or staunch skeptic might ask after viewing this investigation, *"If Billy Graham's Grandfather lived, let's say, a hundred years ago, give or take, how in the world did his ghost learn how to operate a modified EMF detector in order to communicate with you?"* That is a fair question! And we already touched upon this subject in Chapter #3.

The short answer is that we don't know for certain. But we can speculate that once someone leaves this earthly plane of existence and enters the spirit realm, they have access to what has been termed *Universal Intelligence* or *The Morphic Field* (remember those?). It is theorized that there exists a field of knowledge and wisdom that all living beings, including you and I have access to. This isn't science fiction or some fairy tale either. According to quantum physics, there is some scientific basis that all living things are really hooked into one another on a psychic level of sorts. A great example is when a spider builds a web. This small arachnid has hardly any brain to speak of, and yet, when it is only hours old, it is able to build an engineering marvel in a location ideally situated for capturing prey. How is this possible? Scientists theorize that the knowledge is already built into their DNA at some level, but no one has ever been able to look under a microscope and find the tiny spider web blueprints.

That is where the *Morphic Field* theory comes in. It is actually easier, and some would say more logical to assume that they just plug into this field and the knowledge is there. The same as when birds just know when it is time to fly south for the winter. Science calls it *instinct,* which is a term often used to explain the unexplained.

If this truly is the case, and if the process of entering the afterlife frees us from the confines of our skulls. Then it is plausible to assume that we would have access to this limitless intelligence. In turn, this would allow us the ability to instantly learn things. Even how to ping the needle on an EMF detector, or pick the word from an Ovilus type of device (more on the latter in a bit).

A funny side note to this first investigation was that Renee, who was taking the video, thought I was faking the whole communication thing. She thought the Ghost Meter Pro was just a magician's prop. And that I was essentially performing *a magic act* for the camera despite my assurances that I wasn't. It wouldn't be long after this event that Renee would become a believer herself.

Nicky G. sensing something ominous - Ancient Spirit Desires Solitude

Ancient Spirit Desires Solitude

It was early on in our investigations that we actually had our first negative experience. And trust me, it was one that would probably have been the last for most ghost hunting families. But there are several interesting things about it.

In our then hometown of Fort Mill SC there was an ancient 200 year old burial ground named *Old Unity Cemetery*. Though there were no known haunts there, I felt compelled to investigate it. To this day, I cannot think of any spot more haunted. We have captured incredible

81

evidence there including our best EVP to date, but our first visit was anything but welcoming.

Old Unity is a very small place, about half an acre, with most of the stones either illegible or toppled over. Suspiciously large areas dot the land where there weren't any stones at all. I surmised that these were either unmarked graves, or the place where the old church once stood, which could not have been very large. We went there with the GMP around dusk, which by the way we have found is the time with the strongest paranormal activity. Not morning, not the dead of night (pun intended). Dusk, almost always has the most activity, we are still trying to learn why.

We began by looking around the graveyard with the *Phantom Radar app* Nicky G. had installed on her iPhone. This app was the forerunner of all ghost radar apps and was used by experienced paranormal teams according to the information available at the time. The screen on the phone actually looks like a classic radar screen you would see in a submarine. When electromagnetic energy spikes anywhere in a radius around the phone, a "blip" will register on the screen. Once this happens, we head in that direction in the hopes that it is a ghost, which may or may not be the case.

Nicky G. began pacing around the stones when suddenly a blip appeared on the screen. She had never experienced anything like this before so she gasped and literally froze in place. I looked at the screen, and indeed, it appeared we had visitors.

As we headed in the direction dictated by the Phantom Radar, the entire family began to experience a very ominous, heavy feeling. The air became thick and we all felt a bit uneasy. Something we clearly weren't expecting after our last exhilarating investigation.

Just then Courtnee who was holding the GMP got a huge EMF (electromagnetic frequency) spike in the exact spot Nicky G. was detecting a blip which made her jump a mile. *Something was starting to happen.* We switched the GMP into dialogue mode, nothing. Then we did an EVP session, again nothing.

Night continued to fall and the feeling kept getting heavier, again, it wasn't our imagination. We all felt it, and I don't believe in mass hypnosis. We decided to investigate the perimeter of the old burial ground. Again, no luck. So we headed back to the original spot where Courtnee got the huge EMF spike. As soon as we arrived, the blips on the phantom radar vanished, and the GMP went into contact mode.

We had made contact with a ghost. We asked it if it was the spirit of the person on the stone we were standing in front of, *"No"*… Then we asked a few more questions. One was whether or not it was affiliated with the cemetery, *"No"*… Then I asked it if was a good spirit, *"No"*… I started to get cold sweats… Then I asked if it wanted us to leave… The GMP nearly jumped out of my hand when it answered, *"YES"* with a VERY LOUD spike!

You didn't need to tell us twice, we left the cemetery immediately (though we have gone back several times with mind-blowing results). The entire way home the car was quiet, everyone was shaken, we knew that was the real deal.

What was interesting in that early investigation was the fact that it was the first time several pieces of equipment worked in concert with one another validating the presence of an entity. The phantom radar showed a blip, we got an EMF spike in that *exact* spot and nowhere else. Then a communication was triggered, all wrapped up in personal experience in the form of a heavy feeling felt by the four of us. That's four strings of evidence. Now a skeptic would try to debunk each one individually. They would say that the phantom radar is a phone app and therefore unreliable. They would then say that the GMP communication is unproven, (though they would have a little more trouble explaining the EMF spike), and they would say that the personal experience is anecdotal. But when all four pieces of the puzzle fit together perfectly, we have a completed picture so to speak that is hard to dismiss.

When I got back home, I uploaded the complete raw footage to YouTube with no edits, just to see how it looked. I posted a few blurbs about the experience on social media and where people could watch it. After about a week I noticed the video was getting not hundreds, but thousands of views. *It was going viral!* So much so that I knew we had something here. People were intrigued by not only the evidence, but by the family who ghost hunts.

It was then that we thought making a web series would be a novel idea. Renee loved it because the places we were going to, for the most part were historical by nature and thus a great learning experience for the kids. At that point *Gallo Family Ghost Hunters* was officially born.

Television Promotional Banner

6

St. Augustine & Orbs

So with a few investigations under our belt, we decided to head to what we researched as *America's most haunted city*, St. Augustine Florida. And it did not disappoint. These were the investigations where the million dollar question was answered, *Could we catch evidence like the big guys on television?* St. Augustine proved that we could actually catch more.

While in America's oldest city, we were very fortunate to have had the honor and privilege of ghost hunting with one of the most knowledgeable people in the history of the field, The late Dr. Harry Stafford. Who loved our passion for the paranormal, and taught us many things in the short time we had together. Dr. Stafford also validated many of our theories. For that we will be forever grateful.

Here he is teaching Courtnee how to use a thermal gun to check for temperature fluctuations and cold spots in the surroundings.

Courtnee learning from the best... The late Dr. Harry Stafford

Augustine Orb Project

St. Augustine was also the first time we were introduced to a phenomenon that has caused more debate, arguments, and hostility than any other topic in the paranormal field, and still does to this day. *ORBS*, uh oh, I envision the "orb deniers" throwing this book across the room as I write this...tough cookies.

We caught more orbs in St. Augustine than in any other single place we have ever investigated. Why? Good question, but let's examine the subject before we look at the following investigation.

What are Spirit Orbs?

Orbs are those small balls of light that some people catch in images taken with digital cameras, as well as on emulsion film albeit to a much lesser extent. Orb researchers speculate that they are either one of two things;

1. Spirits themselves. There are ancient religious traditions going back centuries which describe orbs in one form or another; such as, a Tibetan Buddhist belief where the orb is a symbol of enlightenment in which the awakened person is reported to have a glow (spirit, aura?) and is symbolized by an orb. Even in our own investigations, we have seen orbs morph into full-body apparitions through a series of photos which we will discuss in the next chapter.
2. They are not spirits in and of themselves, but rather emanations from spirit beings or dimensional portals of sorts.

Orbs are the #1 most controversial and divisive subject in the entire field of paranormal research. If the modern day EVP is the equivalent to the *spirit message* of the Victorian era, then orbs are clearly the *floating trumpets* of today... And are under no less scrutiny.

Skeptics will *go to the mat* kicking and screaming to tell the world that they are caused by dust, pollen, insects, or moisture via a process called *back-scatter*. Which works basically like this, there is a speck of dust (or any one of a number of airborne particles) close to the front of the camera lens. When the flash goes off, the light is reflected off of the particle in question and back to the lens resulting in the image of an orb. That's it! Skeptics have won and the case is closed right? Well, not so fast.

First off, there are particles in the air nearly 100% of the time. They are *always* in front of the camera lens. Yet, orbs appearing at non-haunted locations are relatively rare. I myself have taken several hundred photographs of my new house, *Castello Gallo* with a digital camera and haven't caught one single orb. The house is almost a century old and when I moved in, you can bet there was dust everywhere... But no orbs in any of the photos.

When they do appear, it's almost always at an event where people are gathered such as a celebration, religious ceremony, or conversely, a haunted location. Sound like places a spirit might appear? You betcha!

Our first investigations at *Old Unity Cemetery* ironically revealed few orbs which was odd given the amount of activity we experienced. Yet the cemetery was about as dusty as you could imagine since it was comprised of extremely dry dirt and virtually no grass to speak of. But no orbs at all! So if back-scatter is the be all, end all, explanation, there should have been many! We took the same camera to St. Augustine and we caught dozens of orbs, but not randomly by any means. They only appeared in seriously haunted locations, and when we were communicating with the GMP, and yes, we have photographic proof which we will share with you shortly.

It's also fair to once again point out that manufacturers of the digital camera for the longest time had absolutely no idea where these mysterious orbs were coming from. So being that there was no explanation coming from the camera developers, it wasn't long until a skeptic who couldn't handle the idea of paranormal orbs came up with the "theory" of back-scatter. It was then immediately accepted by the masses of fellow skeptics out there as a plausible debunk. And gave the camera companies a satisfactory explanation for this phenomena. At the risk of repeating myself, what these skeptics also know full well, but fail to tell the public, is the fact that digital cameras can see spectrum of light that the human eye cannot. That is why they can photograph anomaly that cannot be seen with the naked eye. Much in the same way that animals can hear sound wavelength that you nor I can hear.

There are even NASA scientists who do not buy into the back-scatter theory 100%, and have done extensive experimentation to validate the paranormal nature of orbs (see the Orb Project by Klaus Heinemann). And even respected paranormal researchers who are starting to change their minds about the dust theory because true paranormal orbs are all but impossible to replicate (See Fiona Broome, Ghosts, What They are and What They Aren't).

Can airborne particles cause orb-like images?

I feel it appropriate to throw my skeptic friends a bone at this time. Can dust, pollen, lens flare, and moisture cause orb-like anomalies in digital pictures? Yes, absolutely! But these physical objects are readily identified, look nothing like paranormal orbs, and are easily replicated by merely shaking a dusty mop in front of the camera, or running around in the rain if that's what you're into.

Orbs caught on video

Though we have taken hundreds of hours of footage for our web-series, we rarely get orbs on video. However, some people seem to catch dust that look like paranormal orbs in video on a regular basis, and they are quite convincing. So it's important to know what to look for. A good example of genuine spirit orbs caught on video would be the footage we shot on the steps leading up to the balcony of the Palace Theater in Netcong NJ and also in the balcony itself. How do we know these were genuine paranormal orbs? They were also witnessed with the naked eye by Courtnee as we will discuss in chapter #8. So paranormal orbs can indeed be caught on video. Not everything is an airborne contaminant, unless you consider spirit as being such.

What does a paranormal orb actually look like?

The consensus among researchers who specialize in the study of paranormal orbs generally agree on the following two distinct characteristics. One is what some have called a shell or membrane around the perimeter of the orb as seen below. They will also appear to radiate their own light. However, Paranormal orbs can take on other forms as well, but this is by far the most common. It's also the type that is virtually impossible to replicate by orb researchers and skeptics alike.

Empirical evidence of paranormal orbs

Empirical evidence, also known as sense experience, is a collective term for the knowledge or source of knowledge acquired by means of the senses, particularly by observation and experimentation.

In the recommended book *The Orb Project by Klaus Heinemann*, there is mention of an experiment to call a paranormal orb into existence. So being relatively new to the subject we gave it a try. Courtnee wanted to be the one to call the orb so we went out to our back patio in Fort Mill South Carolina, she sat in a chair, concentrated, and called for an orb to appear and pose for a picture. The photo below shows the immediate result.

Now tell me, what are the odds that an orb would show up at the exact moment we requested if this were really an airborne particulate anomaly? One in a million? One in a billion? One in a trillion? At what point does something simply become a statistical impossibility? Unless of course we just accept the existence of the spectral elephant in the room and admit that this just may be a genuine paranormal occurrence.

Courtnee manifesting a large orb (picture enhanced)

Still not convinced? … Courtnee then grabbed her mom's dowsing rods and we conducted the experiment *a second time.* Guess what happened? When we snapped the pic, we noticed that the first orb was still there in the same general location of the frame! But now a second orb appeared at the tips of the dowsing rods that Courtnee was holding where it was apparently influencing communication. We attempted to show you this astonishing picture here but for some inexplicable reason it wouldn't enhance correctly in order to be visible for a book page. But it is available on our *ICOM Paranormal Facebook page* for you to examine along with literally hundreds of other shots from our investigations.

Back-Scatter debunked

I snapped over 300 pictures in St. Augustine, both in infrared and normal modes. Several shots came out completely black, as they were an attempt to photograph the ramparts of the *Castillo de San Marcos* at night (often recognized as one of the most haunted locations in the world). So when I put the pics through a photo editor to lighten them up, this is what I found, a basketball sized orb floating amongst the battlements.

So why am I so sure this wasn't dust? Simple, the original picture was completely black, nothing could be seen. If this was a dust anomaly, the dust would have to be close to the lens. Therefore, when the flash went off, this orb would have been brilliantly illuminated against a dark background. Since it wasn't, by default, it would had to have been be a respectable distance away, too far for the flash to reflect off of it. The orb only became visible after the entire picture was lightened up through our photo editing software. My conclusion is that this orb could not have been an airborne particle. It is exactly what it appears to be.

It's also important to note that *depth perception* plays a huge role in orb validation, and I'm amazed no one ever talks about it. When something is close to the camera lens, it is clearly obvious. It's usually blurry and indistinct. Also obvious when an object is far away. As in the above photo, you can clearly see the distance of the orb, at least I can.

Orb amongst the battlements at the Castillo de San Marcos. This photo was completely black until enhanced with a photo editing program. Only then did the orb appear proving it was too far away to be considered an airborne particle - Augustine Orb Project

Strategic placement

Strategic placement refers to the time when the orb is exactly where it should be, and the odds of it being chance are statistically remote or even impossible. One example was the following picture with Courtnee. But there are others which are equally as astounding.

We suspect that ghosts are electromagnetic in nature. So it stands to reason that orbs may be as well. Notice this incredible picture of the Ghost Meter Pro reacting wildly to the small orb that is near it's tip while Courtnee stands in front of a known haunted structure. Or is this just another dusty coincidence?

Are those intelligent dust balls? - Again, notice the orbs hovering near the Ghost Meter Pro during a spectral communication.

Can dust specks have twin siblings?

We were also privy to a night investigation of the *Castle Warden* in St. Augustine, also known as the *Ripley's Castle.* No place on earth contains more haunted objects (including real shrunken heads). As I wandered off on my own, I snapped a few shots which turned out to contain interesting orbs. If orbs are airborne particles, like snowflakes, no two should ever be alike, right? Isn't it strange then that these two orbs caught in different sections of the same room, in two entirely different shots, have the exact same markings? Wow! That dust ball sure gets around! *sarcasm off* Or conversely, it could be the same spirit orb following me around the Castle. More likely in my opinion.

Notice the "eye" on the left hand side of the orb. Also the horizontal striping. It almost appears to be a floating eyeball. Just saying...

One of the prime debunks orb skeptics love to use is the false notion that you cannot take two pictures of the same orb. Therefore, it has to be dust, moisture, or pollen. Well, guess what? Could this be considered *repeatable scientific evidence?*

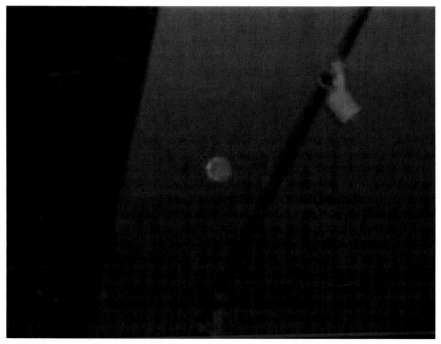

This orb has all the same characteristics as the first one. In fact, a close examination will show that it's identical. Also, it wasn't in any other additional photos. This presents a clear statistical impossibility that it could have been an airborne particle. Finally, let's not forget where this was taken, which was in the great hall of "The Castle Warden" which is notoriously haunted.

Despite all of the evidence and sheer logic that has been presented, the majority of orb deniers will steadfastly stand their ground and look the other way. It's a shame really. They are missing out on evidence that is literally staring them in the face. Paranormal anomalies that are showing themselves and saying *"Here I am!"* And that may be part of the problem. I think that many paranormal investigators cannot accept the fact that evidence like this can be captured by the normal everyday person with a digital camera. Because if that is the case, then the *elite* paranormal investigators with all of their expensive gear, miles of cable, and matching *Ghost Buster* team uniforms aren't the special people they want *The Travel Channel* or *Destination America* to think they are.

Same goes with cell phone apps. In the eyes of the skeptic or the individuals with cool initials after their name signifying that they are *certified paranormal investigators*, it's blasphemy to be able to capture paranormal evidence with something everyone has access to and only costs a few bucks… BTW, who certifies these people anyway?

I also remember having a conversation with an orb skeptic who said that it was impossible to capture dust orbs with infrared photography due to the absence of flash needed for the back-scatter theory to work. Then I presented him with orbs I captured in IR and all of a sudden the conversation changed. Now, according to him, it was possible to catch dust with IR as well. There is no way to placate this type of person. And this person seems to get around.

I think the herd mentality also has much to do with this jaded attitude. For example, there was a self-proclaimed paranormal expert who, not too long ago, stated that it was illogical for ghosts to haunt cemeteries, and therefore said locations could not produce reliable evidence. This is complete and utter nonsense! Cemeteries are some of the most haunted locations in the world, and some are literal "hotbeds" of paranormal activity. *"We should know!"* But when this respected man made that statement, I had very intelligent friends who took it as gospel and argued with me all day long that I was wasting my time despite the fact that we as a team were getting some of our *greatest evidence* from *haunted cemeteries!* It's the blind leading the blind syndrome, or the stubborn leading the stubborn. One of the two I'm sure.

I feel it is the same with orbs. Once the back-scatter theory became widespread, and a few *know-it-all's* produced YouTube videos showing their dust balls to everyone. This type of evidence *was done for* in the eyes of the more skeptical investigators. They will never admit that they were wrong no matter how compelling the evidence, or how logical the existence of paranormal orbs are when properly analyzed, but that is their prerogative.

Finally, some skeptics will maintain that when a picture surfaces that has dozens of orbs in it; they "must" be airborne particles by default as there could not possibly be that many spirits in one picture. You will hear snarky comments spewing from them that go something like this, *"Wow, that's a really dusty room you have there,"* or *"Someone needs a dust-buster."* They actually use the multiple orb shots as a reason to debunk the picture despite the fact that they can never explain how some people get no orbs in one shot, immediately followed by a shot with dozens in the same frame, followed again by a shot having no orbs at all, all in rapid succession.

However, to reiterate what I stated at the start of this section, it is actually theorized by some, that orbs may not be ghosts at all, but *emanations* from spirit. Hence a single spirit may be able to produce multiple orbs. Just giving you all sides of the picture here. Blind belief may not be good when it comes to paranormal investigation, but blind skepticism doesn't help anyone either.

Spirit In The Forgotten Town Square

Orbs were really just the tip of the iceberg when it came to the massive amounts of evidence captured at St. Augustine Florida. Such as, mysterious *ecto-plasma* type haze gradually forming in our infrared shots at the site of the old Menorcan town square in the historical section of St. Augustine where hangings allegedly took place. This mist was not visible to the naked eye. But we could literally see it in the viewing screen of the camera as we took the shots.

This event was actually part of an investigative walking tour conducted by Dr. Harry Stafford that we will never forget. We have several impressive videos on our channel from that incredible evening.

But the supreme highlight of the night for me, was when we made contact with an entity through the Ghost Meter Pro which Dr. Stafford participated in by asking the questions. Something tells me he didn't know quite what to make of the GMP, but he seemed to believe what happened was genuine. Which is common. Many times it takes a personal experience to become convinced. Though, I am certain that I could investigate for the next century and probably not have as many paranormal experiences as Dr. Stafford.

Interesting side note to this investigation: Midway through the GMP communication one of our party asked the spirit a question in Spanish and the response was correct! ... Apparently *Menorca Island* is indeed a part of Spain.

St. Augustine Ghost Crawl

After the experience at the Menorcan square, we were taken to the *Old Huguenot Cemetery* by Dr. Stafford which boasts a myriad of hauntings. Battery drain, orbs, as well as full body apparitions are quite common there.

The cemetery actually sits beside a busy roadway which can be very distracting and annoying, as well as making it nearly impossible to get any good EVP. But even though the mood of the investigation was compromised, that didn't stop the activity in this historic and very haunted patch of land.

By this time we had made friends with another ghost hunting family during this investigative tour and it was fun watching them analyze everything we did. To them we appeared to be experienced paranormal investigators. That wasn't the case by a long shot. We were just passionate about what we were discovering.

As soon as Nicky G. approached the gate to the burial ground, her Ghost Meter Pro which was set to regular EMF mode started to react, something was definitely there. We filmed this investigation entirely in infrared in the hopes of catching something that could not be seen within the normal spectrum of human vision. Nothing was caught on video this time, so whatever was making our equipment "light up" remained a mystery. However, we did get some strategically placed orbs in many of our shots around the headstones and monuments.

Dr. Stafford then led us to a Native American burial site that was located underneath a parking lot. Talk about a recipe for paranormal activity! While there, we seemed to communicate with an ancient American Indian spirit connected to the site and apparently happy to still be there. Once again, Dr. Stafford as well as our new found friends were eager to ask questions through the GMP which the ghost graciously answered. Some of the answers were very surprising and unexpected. Courtnee at the time was busy attempting to see if there were any temperature fluctuations or cold spots near the spot where we were communicating. She was learning faster than any of us!

Next was *Tolomato Cemetery*. Twice during our trip, we had immense activity at the gates of this cemetery. Unfortunately, the gates were locked and we could not enter. But that didn't keep us from detecting unusual psychic energy as well as mysterious orbs that circled Courtnee's GMP once we conducted evidence review of these very compelling photographs (see above).

We switched the GMP into dialogue mode and it triggered almost immediately. Dr. Stafford had been telling us the tale of *James Morgan*. A boy who was buried behind the tall black iron gates and whose spirit is often seen in the branches of the large tree just inside the entrance. The communication suggested that it was him and that he wasn't happy with people visiting his resting place.

This short 7 minute episode is literally packed with gold nuggets, not the least of which is the chance to see Dr. Harry Stafford in action. God rest his soul.

Serious Ghost Hunters in Action - St. Augustine Ghost Crawl

Real Ghost Accepts A Challenge

The following night we ventured out on our own without the expertise of Dr. Stafford. We remembered some of the locations he introduced us to on the tour, so we revisited some of those active *hot-spots* with our gear.

Our perseverance seemed to be rewarded when we had a spirit accept a challenge at the *Old Pour House* which we were told was a tavern closed due to intense paranormal activity (though I heard that since our investigation it has reopened).

This is also a good time to mention that this was also the location of a shadow person apparition sighting the previous night. Several of our investigative tour group saw the shadow figure with their own eyes in the top window of the closed building. So as quickly as I could, I turned my camera up to the window and took several shots. To our collective amazement, in the first picture, you can clearly see a black human figure standing in front of the window. In subsequent pictures it was gone. Plus, the open door you see in the upstairs window, closed by it's own accord.

For the sake of clarity the shadow figure has been outlined. It's also important to note that in subsequent pictures it vanished and the door closed. The bright orb hovering around the window may have been a mere coincidence, Or not.

When we arrived back at the spot, we started the investigation by cautiously approaching the building. As soon as we were approximately 3 feet from the structure, Courtnee began to get crazy high EMF readings on her detector. Which was odd since the building was closed up and had no active power whatsoever as stated by Dr. Stafford. When I tried to do the same thing the EMF spikes ceased which is not at all surprising since Courtnee always seems to get more activity than I do! Then Nicky G. tried and guess what happened? Her detector began sensing what appeared to be ghostly energy!

So on a hunch I asked whatever entity might be there to approach my detector and lo and behold, the detector went off! We played this game several times with the phantom despite rude passerby's mocking what we were doing. If they only knew, they probably wouldn't sleep for the next month!

I vividly remember that when this happened, I thought we would never get evidence as convincing as this again, Boy was I wrong! The unfortunate thing about this episode is that the bulk of the footage we captured during a very critical Ghost Meter Pro dialogue mysteriously vanished off of the video disk.

To cap it all off, Nicky G's camera refused to work when it came anywhere near the building. I examined it as did Renee, and we both confirmed that it was inoperative. However, as soon as we left the area and walked nearly a block from the structure, it suddenly became functional again.

Nicky G. detecting EMF where there should be none - Real Ghost Accepts A Challenge

Shadow Soldier Sighting At The Castillo de San Marcos

The *Castillo de San Marcos* is the oldest fort in the continental United States, located on the western shore of Matanzas Bay. The *Castillo* was designed by the Spanish engineer Ignacio Daza beginning in 1672. On touring the massive structure, you can almost feel the ancient energy. Especially around the *execution wall* where you can still see the holes in the stone left by old musket balls. Dr. Stafford told me that it was probably one of the most haunted locations in the country, if not the world. I think he was right.

It was in this location that the kids had the greatest paranormal experience of the entire trip. A *full body apparition* witnessed by both Nicky G. and Courtnee in one of the turrets of the Castillo de San Marcos which at the time, was invisible to Renee and myself. It's quite an odd experience when you are standing right beside those are seeing something that you cannot. It also speaks to the age old belief that the young can more readily see the supernatural than those who reach maturity due to the fact that they are far more open to such things. As you get older and your belief systems change, so does your perception of the paranormal. This dynamic may also be responsible for the fact that skeptics have a much harder time gathering paranormal evidence than those who accept it's existence in the first place.

Unfortunately, we didn't get the apparition nor the live sighting on video. It was too spontaneous and we simply didn't have the camera running at the time, but we did capture the entire experience on audio. So we produced the episode as a slide-show. It remains one of my of my absolute favorites despite it's simplicity.

Recordings and slides of this event can be found on our web-series channel at: www.ghosthunter.ws

7

The Haunted Carolina's

O ur video views on YouTube were exploding, and we were getting noticed by many people including paranormal teams all across the world. We were getting invitations to England to join investigations in haunted castles, our fan base was building, and we even got invited on a television game show all expenses paid. But we declined this offer when we learned that we would be crawling through mud and things like that, no thanks.

Then suddenly, the unexpected happened. We were subsidizing our investigation travel expenses with the scant monies that were being generated on our YouTube channel. But despite all of our efforts to comply with YouTube guidelines, our monetization was pulled. We were informed that we were cancelled due to *click fraud*, a fate worse than death for many content creators at the time.

We suspect it was a rival paranormal team who wasn't too happy with our new found success *spam clicking* our videos. An underhanded tactic that has ruined the YouTube careers of many honest people. And though we tried to explain how we were operating our show well within site guidelines, YouTube remained stubborn, and our monetization on that network remains disabled to this day, over seven years later.

As fate would have it, a new paranormal network reached out to us called *GTN (Ghost Tales Network) America's Paranormal Superstation.* They placed our entire series in a prime-time line-up, it was a prestigious place to be. The only problem was that we needed to supply our own advertisers in order to raise funds for investigations which were becoming costly.

So while keeping our videos on the GTN station line-up, we looked for another platform where we could monetize the series, this is where *Blip.tv* came in. Blip was an upcoming web-series platform that was attracting not only content creators like ourselves, but popular Hollywood celebrities who saw that television quality web-series were the entertainment wave of the future.

GTN (Ghost Tales Network) America's Paranormal Superstation Promo

Our series became a smash hit on Blip.tv, so much so that we were *awarded* a premium page position. This was only bestowed upon the best of the best. We had premium placement in the channel line-up, advertisers, as well as a robust producer suite which ultimately translated into desperately needed funds. The future was looking bright indeed! Unfortunately for everyone involved, Blip.tv folded after about one year and we were left looking for yet another video platform for the show.

The next stop on the video platform train brought us to *Dailymotion* who immediately assigned us a personal assistant due to our popularity and large fan base. They imported our videos onto their platform, and embedded our episodes globally on portal sites they owned. Also, since Dailymotion was accessible as a ROKU and Amazon Fire TV channel, we were officially an independent TV Show, much in the same way an internet radio show is considered a viable *radio show* itself. In the beginning of our relationship with Dailymotion, we were getting thousands upon thousands of views. Clearly the most we had experienced up to that time. The channel looked great and it seemed that we had found our permanent home.

Unfortunately, just as this book was ready to go to print, Dailymotion had a policy change which has been updated to state that *UFO and paranormal events* are now considered *sensitive topics* and are no longer eligible for ad revenue generation, you can't make this stuff up folks.

So, picking up the pieces once again, I produced two video explanations to our fans, one geared to YouTube and one for Dailymotion viewers explaining why we are now migrating from Dailymotion to our new and hopefully final home... *Vimeo.*

Vimeo is quite a different animal from both YouTube and it's European counterpart, Dailymotion. For starters... With Vimeo, you don't get paid to be part of the network, you pay them instead. Now why on earth would anyone want to do that? Well, for several very good reasons. First, we now have no restrictions and can run our own commercials on the network. We can now market the book you are reading, our affiliate links for paranormal gear, swag, special edition programs that may be of interest to serious paranormal investigators such as uncut footage that they can download and analyze, you name it. Because we now own the channel and are not bound by restrictive advertiser policies or how many times someone watches a video.

All of the episodes are now streamed in broadcast quality high definition. No more compressed, fuzzy looking episodes. They now look like genuine television shows as intended. And speaking of TV shows, Vimeo actually functions as a launching pad and hosting platform for the production of ROKU and Amazon Fire TV channels. Which now is my ultimate goal... *G.F.G.H TV*... You heard it here first.

Haunted Rosedale Plantation

Initially, while all of the YouTube action was happening, we investigated numerous *active* locations all over the Carolinas, such as the *Historic (Haunted) Rosedale Plantation.* Called one of the most haunted houses in the South, with no less than five different ghosts sighted at various times.

For the most part, during the beginning of the investigation, we saw very little activity. We explored the old house beginning with the attic where we came across a very old, and very creepy wooden cradle. We switched on the Ghost Meter Pro and put it in dialogue mode. It searched and searched but *never triggered* despite Courtnee's best efforts at sweeping the entire area. There were virtually no detectable energies in the attic.

So we worked our way down to the basement. Dodging tourists who were touring the house for more historical reasons. There we met a wonderful local woman named Millie. When we asked her about the ghosts who were said to roam Historic Rosedale, she sat down and told us the tale of a man named Jeff who would open a small door built into one of the posts on the back porch to use the shaving supplies that were stored there many years ago. He used these supplies to help shave his friend Baxter who was crippled in the Civil War. The latter who's wheelchair was predominantly displayed in the same room as Millie (2020 hindsight, I should have checked that wheelchair for EMF energy).

To this day, Jeff's ghost supposedly still opens the small door in the post looking for the shaving supplies and leaves it that way every morning despite being closed up again every evening by the Rosedale staff. So dutifully, we made a beeline to that spot and found the haunted niche Millie spoke about. We turned on our GMP and this time, rather than searching endlessly as it had in the attic, it triggered almost immediately. After which we had an insightful conversation with the ghost of Jeff who admitted that he was the one who opens the small door daily. Even in the afterlife he maintains his daily ritual of shaving Baxter.

If you go ahead and look up this episode, during the opening slide show, see if you can locate the two faint orbs (taken without a flash) in two of the rooms. We never noticed them until years later. Also, you can experience the rare treat of hearing the entire tale of Jeff and Baxter from Millie herself.

Nicky G. feeling strange vibrations at Haunted Rosedale Plantation

Messages From The Crypt

This short episode took place at *Bell Tower Park in Salisbury NC*. The reason we chose this city was simple. They offered an evening ghost walking tour which are always a great way to get *leads* whenever you are in a strange city. They are usually held at night and sometimes, even by candlelight, which adds a chilling dimension to the stories of the area. I look at them as a way to ghost hunt without the attempt to make contact with an entity which admittedly isn't for everyone. Some tours like the one Dr. Harry Stafford conducted, will actually lend you paranormal gear and train you in their use.

Often times we would sign-up for these tours and then strike out on our own to re-visit and investigate the areas described after the walk was over. This turned out to be very fruitful when we toured Salisbury. The city was loaded with haunted locations. Most of them could only be looked at from a distance. And for the most part, the buildings on the tour were inaccessible, to me that was the frustrating part.

Nicky G. opened this episode with a recap of what we experienced on the ghost-walk the night before. We scoured the park area just as the bell in the tower began to toll. It made the atmosphere perfect for a ghost hunt.

We then stumbled upon what was probably the strangest location we have ever encountered. Underneath the old meeting house in the center of Bell Tower Park, we encountered a number of eerie above ground crypts behind wrought iron bars. Using the Ghost Speaker app, words began coming through that indicated a festival or wedding of some sort. I later made the connection that weddings must have been held in the meeting house directly above the crypts. Leaving us with a perfect example of relevance in ghost hunting.

During this investigation, we also connected with a spirit named Catherine Chambers, who almost succeeded in helping us solve the mystery of who lies in the one *unknown* grave beneath the meeting house.

The eerie above ground crypts underneath the old meeting house -
Messages From The Crypt

Let's talk a bit about relevance

Relevance is one of the most important key factors in paranormal
investigation and ghost hunting. It's what glues the separate pieces of
evidence together into a complete picture.

When we use equipment such as the Ghost Speaker or conduct a
Ghost Box session. If the words make no sense, we have no choice but
to chalk the communication up to random EMF triggering the words
in a haphazard manner on the phone's magnetometer. Or in the case
of a Ghost Box, the radio sweep just happens to capture broadcasts

118

that have nothing at all to do with the paranormal.

However, if the words *begin to come together in a thematic relationship*, especially when they coincide with the location, event, or specific ghost we are attempting to communicate with, then it's time to get excited! It's at this point we may have the makings of a genuine paranormal or psychic communication. Couple that with a photographic anomaly, EVP, personal experience, cold spots, or other types of evidence, and the validity of the scenario as a whole starts to become conclusive.

Looking back, what was absolutely astounding, was the sheer fact that, overall, we were capturing evidence on virtually every single investigation! It was becoming so commonplace that even other paranormal groups had no idea how we were doing it. And it wasn't just Ghost Meter Pro sessions. We were getting mind-altering EVP, photographic anomaly, and just about everything else our equipment was able to capture. And some it wasn't even meant to capture. We just chalked it up to the fact that we were so respectful and unique among ghost hunters that spirits were naturally drawn to us and thus willing to communicate.

Alone In A Dark Cemetery

Clearly the best pieces of equipment are the ones specifically designed for paranormal research. While some are better than others, every once in awhile a piece of equipment comes along that provides really solid evidence. One such piece of equipment is *The Spirit Touch*. Only a very limited number of these units were made and I was lucky enough to get my hands on one. It works via the same process as the touch screen on a cell phone. Using an exchange of electrons, someone or something has to touch the little yellow pad on the face in order for the small LED light to either go on or off depending on how you set it. It was designed so that it could not be triggered by outside interference or random EMF.

We continued to explore the city of Salisbury in search of the most haunted locations we could find. My family was literally fearless. Ghosts were out there, they wanted to find them, and find them we did.

During the tour, our guide recommended an old confederate cemetery that dated back to 1768 as a very active location. So after the tour was over, we made our way back. The area was questionable and I didn't feel very comfortable there. Especially since it was now late at night and far off the beaten path. We also had to conduct the investigation outside of the cemetery as to not violate town laws forbidding entry into a cemetery after dark.

In Fiona Broome's excellent book, *Ghost Hunting in Haunted Cemeteries*, she states that cemetery gates are often the most haunted parts of the burial ground. And this investigation certainly seemed to prove that beyond a reasonable doubt.

We began off to the side of the cemetery near a secondary gate and conducted a *base-line reading* of the gates and the connected stone wall to confirm that there was no inherent EMF in the area. There was a clear absence of power lines which I also looked for in order to rule out any possibility that the EMF could come from above should we have a spike.

Nicky G. attempted an EVP session but to no avail. Then upon Renee's advice, we made our way around to the main gate where we began to get moderate EMF readings. I then broke out the Spirit Touch and attempted to use it simultaneously with the Ghost Meter Pro. This is a technique I often use to see if evidence on one piece of equipment can be validated on another.

Before long, the GMP triggered into communication mode at the old iron gates. The entity, when asked if it could touch the little yellow area on the Spirit Touch pinged a *"No"* answer. Sure enough, nothing at all happened on the Spirit Touch. So even though we didn't get hard evidence on the Spirit Touch in terms of the LED blinking off, it was interesting to note that the spirit present indeed said that it wouldn't touch the device. This may not have been ground breaking validation. But it all fit together and made perfect sense. And just as a quick FYI, we have had the Spirit Touch activate without any questions being asked during other investigations. It does seem as though it takes a certain amount of effort on the part of a ghost to manifest enough to make actual contact with the *touch zone* on the Spirit Touch. Which may be why some spirits can do it and others can't. Still others may be hesitant to interact with the unit for any number of unknown reasons.

Courtnee and Renee comparing evidence - Alone In A Dark Cemetery

Unknown Soldiers

One of the things we get criticized for from the hard-core paranormal community is the fact that we use licenced background music to set the mood in our episodes. This is admittedly done for production value. But there are fans out there who will turn up the volume and listen intently during our episodes in order to catch anomaly. I have to admit that they have a point. But the goal here is two-fold. To capture evidence is number one, but also to retain an audience. And that's not going to happen when it appears that the only thing we are doing is posting home-movies. With that in mind, this next episode had some very nice military style music in honor of those we contacted.

During this particular time, Nicky G. was in high school ROTC, so naturally it seemed like a great time to visit *Salisbury National Cemetery*. Nicky G. took total command of this episode. She was in her element and knew exactly how to conduct this investigation.

The activity during the initial half of the ghost hunt was virtually non-existent. But that all changed when Courtnee began reading the history of the area on the informational podium near the central monument. Immediately blips started to come through on the Ghost Radar app as though she caught someones attention. As the entities approached, much of our equipment ceased to function. It seemed they were obliging us by siphoning the energy from our electronics.

At first Courtnee seemed nervous. We could literally feel them surrounding us. But once I explained to her that these were the ghosts of the nation's fallen, she eased up and so did the atmosphere. The spirits realized our intentions were honorable and seemed appreciative that we were there in a respectful way.

Judging by the GMP communication, the spirit of one unknown soldier in particular who appeared to be a Marine, responded well to Nicky G's *"Oorah!"* Marine motivational call. To validate this, I used a hand held EMF detector app (*it was the Ghost-O-Meter*). The needle would jump when Nicky G. would gave them that call.

We had several communications, physical sensations, as well as catching a stunning EVP that appeared to be an entire platoon echoing Nicky G's salute to them! They appeared to shout, *"Oorah!"* or *"Hooray"*… Not entirely sure which. This EVP blew away very respected people in the paranormal field such as April Abercrombie of *Ghost Advice* who said that it actually sounded like an entire platoon saluting us.

The moment we realized that a platoon of spirits were surrounding us -
Unknown Soldiers

British Ghost Soldier Gallops Again

The evidence continued to pile-up, not to mention video footage. Communication with entities on any given investigation as well as captured paranormal images almost felt commonplace. Which in retrospect is still quite curious given our relatively brief track-record in the field at that time. But up until that point we still hadn't captured anything that was knocking our socks off until our visit to this historical location.

Kings Mountain was the site of a pivotal battle in the Revolutionary war with over 300 men buried where they fell. The accounts of hauntings are numerous. But the most famous phenomenon people experience there are the ghostly galloping sounds of a *Phantom Horseman.*

This episode marked the first time Renee appeared on camera much to the delight of our growing fan base. I mean, just look at her, she's gorgeous. The camera clearly loves her. And as fate would have it, it was also the first time she would have a tactile experience with a spirit.

We began by trekking up and down the paths, getting some blips on the Phantom Radar as well as brief EMF spikes, but nothing to write home about. Courtnee running ahead of us the entire time. Most of the landmarks were in the middle of the woods so non-paranormal EMF would have been ultra rare. Good thing we all had comfortable sneakers on.

We continued through the park via a winding path when suddenly, it happened. I stopped the group when I heard it, as clear as day, up and off to my right, it was the galloping of *The Phantom Horseman of Kings Mountain!*

Much like the time when Nicky G. and Courtnee were the only ones who witnessed the full-body apparition in the tower of the *Castillo de San Marcos in St. Augustine.* It was I who was the only person on the team to experience the famous galloping phenomenon that the battlefield was known for. The fantastic thing was, not only did I experience it, but we got it all on our digital EVP recorder which we had recording at the time. One of the very best EVP ever recorded in my extremely biased opinion, eclipsed by only one other that we will be talking about very soon.

Just after that happened, Renee felt a spirit touch her on the arm that was holding the camera. At first she dismissed it, then it happened a second time, confirming her suspicions that something was actually following us through the battlefield which was validated by the readings on the Phantom Radar.

We then approached a small wooden bridge where we caught the strangest sound on our EVP recorder. It was the sound of a heavy wooden chest (or door) creaking open. It was an unmistakable sound that was only captured on the digital recorder. We heard nothing at the time with our own ears.

This investigation was also the first time Renee had the chance to communicate with an entity through the GMP. Up to this point she still thought I was doing something to manipulate the device for showmanship purposes. This time, she held it herself, and experienced what the kids and I were experiencing every time the GMP triggered into dialogue mode.

Our spectral hiking companion appeared to be the wandering spirit of a soldier who was killed at Kings Mountain. The soldier seemed to communicate that he was a British loyalist who actually became quite angry when we told him that Renee was French! Soon after that bombshell revelation the communication ceased. Renee finally became convinced, this wasn't a toy, this was real, and it was a rush!

After this compelling ethereal conversation we all sat down on some large rocks for some ghost hunt debriefing which we taped for the show. Nicky G. related to us that she felt dizzy and drained after the communication. It may have been that the spirit was using her personal energy in order to communicate with us.

Renee experiencing her first spirit communication - British Ghost Soldier Gallops Again

Return To Kings Mountain

A number of episodes later, we actually did a follow-up investigation of Kings Mountain Battlefield. It was on this investigation we clearly confirmed that a ghost hunt doesn't necessarily need to be in the evening, in the dark, or during a storm in order to catch paranormal evidence (though those things *might* help). Whether most were residual haunts, or intelligent haunts, we don't know for sure, but that battlefield was *hot* as we like to say in the paranormal biz, and deserved another look.

For the second time it seemed like an entity was actually following us down the path. When we arrived at *Col. Ferguson's* grave, which was now a high mound of rock built to protect his remains, we caught an EVP that said *"Get Up There Kid"*... Presumably asking one of the kids to climb the mound, which wasn't going to happen on my watch. But it's interesting to note the many EVP we have caught over the course of our investigations that specifically mention the kids in one form or another. After that EVP we soon got another which wasn't a word, but an actual *"giggle."*

But the best was yet to come. While exploring up on top of the ridge opposite the spot where I heard it last, the *galloping phantom horseman* was again heard. But this time by *both* Renee and myself, and because of our positioning, I now know the general area where the manifestation occurs.

During our first investigation I was on the bottom of the ridge and the sound came from just above me on the ridge. We were now on top of the ridge and the sound was coming from the exact direction of where I was standing the last time. Which means that the phantom gallop manifests somewhere in the middle of those two spots!

As a bonus,we also got this AVP on video, twice! Once through our main camera, and again through the HD video sunglasses I was wearing. Though faint, it can still be heard. This event was also validated by the Ghost Radar which prior to this event, generated a word that said *"Listen"* just before we heard the horseman, you can't get better validation than that.

We closed the episode with a combination GMP/EVP session that was unnerving. When we asked the entities who were following us to ping the needle on the GMP, an EVP came though that asked, *"How?"*It turned out that he was a loyalist soldier who was trapped at the battlefield. When we asked, we got an affirmative on the GMP and immediately an EVP that said *"Here."*

Then came the gut wrenching part, when Renee asked if we could do anything for him an EVP came through that said very clearly, *"Help me out of here."* Just as the needle pinged *"Yes"* on the GMP. I didn't know how to respond to this, so I just asked the first thing that came to mind and that was if he wanted us to pray for him. The GMP responded with a loud *"NO,"* as he abruptly left.

Nicky G. pondering what awaits us inside the imposing Masonic Temple - Temple Spirits

We Were Not Alone - The Greatest EVP Ever Caught

EVP (electromagnetic voice phenomenon) has always been possible to an extent with old style tape recorders. But today's digital recorders have a sensitivity and ability to record spectrum of audio far superior to that of old school magnetic tape. And they keep getting better and more sensitive as time goes on. This is the one type of evidence that rarely gets knocked by skeptics unless the words are so unintelligible that they chalk it up to either pareidolia, or sound contamination from the surroundings. The latter of which is a risk that actually increases with the newer ultra-sensitive recorders.

The EVP recorded in the following investigation was actually caught by mistake! That's right, we had no idea we were about to record an EVP that is so haunting, once a person hears it, they may have trouble sleeping for the next several days... Or longer.

Renee and I returned to *Old Unity Cemetery* despite our previous experience there to test a new piece of gear out (yes, the place we were told to leave by a ghost). We thought the investigation was a total failure; however, the only failure was by us realizing that we never turned off our handheld digital recorder. Which ironically, resulted in one of our greatest success stories as ghost hunters!

As I went up to my office at home, I finally realized that my trusty RCA digital recorder was still on, so I downloaded the file to my PC where I noticed some unusual sound waves on my *Audacity* sound editing program. So I played the clip and listened intently, at first I was laughing while listening to Renee and myself tripping all over the place in an attempt to get out of the cemetery before nightfall.

Then suddenly, a third voice came into the recording while Renee and

I were talking. It was very clear that it was speaking on a different frequency entirely. In fact, it seemed to be whispering very close to the mic on the recorder. It was a wispy, ethereal female voice saying, *"Come Back!"…"Don't Leave Now"…* I sat there in stunned shock. Feel free to go to our channel and listen for yourself, but don't say I didn't warn you.

We made several trips back to Old Unity, each time we captured new and unique evidence. The Southern USA is an incredible place, so much history and as many ghosts. Here are more highlights.

Eager Ghost Communication

So we once again went back to Old Unity, despite lack of hospitality shown to us by a spirit the last time the whole family was there and took the Spirit Touch with us this time around. By this time we were a bit sharper and braver. Plus we were confident that we would get evidence here and that is why we were doing this in the first place.

It seemed as though our ethereal friends were expecting us. No sooner did we enter the cemetery, our fully-charged main video camera died. Completely drained of all power. So we resorted to using the video on one of our cell phones which was still working.

Courtnee started getting readings on her EMF almost immediately which was expected. Nicky G. was on EVP duty, Renee was on (cell phone) camera, and I broke out the Spirit Touch which to my surprise, went off in my hand. But I debunked that as my own energy interfering with the unit somehow. So I reset the unit and placed it upon the fallen grave stone of what we felt was the most active grave in the cemetery. And the one whom we suspect gave us our stunning

EVP, the grave of Nancy.

We backed well away from the grave, and before I could even stop talking (which is quite hard for me) it worked. When we asked the spirit to touch the yellow contact zone, the *LED dramatically switched itself off* as we all got the collective chills. Immediately following that, the GMP went into communication mode confirming that the spirit communicating with us was indeed Nancy.

Plus, as usual, upon reviewing the still photos taken during the communication with Courtnee, the orbs caught were hovering specifically around the Ghost Meter Pro. Also, in successive shots, orbs were photographed in the same positions twice. Ruling out the possibility that they could have been dust or pollen. It's also interesting to note that orbs appear in no other photos that evening. Which abruptly ended when the rest of our equipment suddenly died like our video camera, time to leave, again.

Attempting to photograph an entity during Nicky G's EVP session - Eager Ghost Communication

Ghost Voices In The Machine

We only went back to Old Unity Cemetery one more time for this short episode before we decided to give the spirits there a break. We wanted to do a follow-up after the mind-blowing, thematic evidence we obtained on our last visit. By now the spirits that either resided or visited that area seemed more than happy to have us there, no threatening vibes whatsoever.

I actually was told by Robert Grote. A paranormal friend of mine who is a shaman of sorts and Reiki Master that this burial ground was the location of a spiritual *vortex* which was why we normally got so much intense activity here. But not this time. We felt that this visit was a total waste of time as it was frustratingly quiet. Nothing seemed to be happening. Were the spirits of the place ignoring us so we would stop pestering them?

However, upon evidence review, we learned that we had captured two Class-A EVPs, one male and one female. When we asked the entity to assist us in communicating via a certain piece of equipment, the EVP asked *"How?"* Finally, I said to Renee that I had never seen it so quiet. Just then an EVP came though that said, *"Never."* Which seemed to be mocking me by repeating what I said.

This investigation also confirmed to us what we've always suspected; we seem to get the most activity when investigating around dusk.

Temple Spirits 1 & 2

We were hitting our stride. The more experience we gained at ghost hunting, the better we got at capturing compelling evidence. So we looked for better and more intense places to investigate in the hopes of experiencing apparitions or minor poltergeist activity. So I did some research and found a haunted Masonic Lodge in Asheville North Carolina that was willing to allow us free reign to investigate. It was tough enough finding good indoor investigations, so this was an offer we couldn't refuse.

Asheville NC is a historic town that hosts a wide diversity of people, including witches. We were informed that there were many haunted spots in the area; especially notable were the enormous Masonic Lodge and Riverside Cemetery which were known to be incredibly active. We started with the Masonic Lodge investigation. I was enthralled with the structure which was riddled with secret rooms and multiple floors containing every kind of Masonic secret.

We spent a good amount of time outside of the Temple mentally preparing ourselves for the ghost hunt to follow. We were also waiting for our guide to arrive to let us in, so we made the best of it by creating a few videos expressing our thoughts about what was to be our first evening *lock down* inside of a notably haunted structure. As expected, Courtnee took center stage here. In fact, I recently unearthed this footage and released it in the form of a short featurette. The cuteness factor is just off the charts.

Our guide on this investigation introduced us to a haunted ceremonial sword. At first I was skeptical, but I soon found out that it held an incredible EMF charge no one could explain. We then obtained several Class-A EVP in the basement, and experienced a ghost who was willing to walk right up to my EMF detector and back again upon request many times. This is a phenomenon we have experienced frequently and caught on video in several episodes. It truly is some of the most convincing evidence as it shows intelligent communication. Not residual energy, and certainly not random. This investigation was also to be the first time Nicky G. was actually touched on the hand by a spirit. This wasn't surprising. Our guide, though a Mason and member of the lodge himself, was allowing us to venture into places that were normally forbidden to those who were not Masons themselves. Actions like this are bound to stir up energies and that is exactly what seemed to be happening.

The highlight of the evening seemed to be the communication with a deceased *Grand Master Mason* which blew our young guide away. He later told us on tape that it was the best investigation at the temple he had ever seen. It was just another day for us, I also think he had a crush on Nicky G.

Nicky G. and Courtnee bravely experiencing paranormal activity in the basement of the Asheville Masonic Temple during our very first "Black-Out" investigation. - Temple Spirits

Grave Matters - The phone app that named the dead

It was the cemetery investigation that turned out to produce the most mind-blowing evidence of the entire trip to Asheville NC. In fact, this investigation alone puts to rest the debate on whether or not paranormal cell phone apps have merit, I think you will agree.

136

Riverside Cemetery was recommended by our Masonic tour guide Tadd, who told us that there were numerous reports of paranormal activity there. Nothing specific, but we didn't care, the mere *possibility* of ghosts or spirits at a given location has always been enough for us. So we geared up and drove over.

What struck us from the outset was the large number of Masonic tombstones. Many Masonic lodges for some odd reason were known to be haunted, including the one we had just investigated. And it seemed that Asheville was a haven for Masons over the past century and a half due to what we were seeing here, as some of the stones with Masonic symbols inscribed on them were quite old. Perhaps there was some connection with the paranormal activity experienced at this site and the number of Masons buried here?

Upon exploring this large city of the dead we happened upon a huge stone mausoleum built into the hillside. There were no names on it, or markings of any kind other than what appeared to be a German style iron cross above the entrance way, and an ornate letter R on the large marble doors. What made this a strange experience however, were what appeared to be *bloodstains* on the door. Upon effecting research, I found out that this was the Rumbough-Baker mausoleum. The crypt was designed by inventor John Baker for his family. His son-in-law, James T. Rumbough, was the first (and only) mayor of Montford. For that reason, the iron hasp on the front of the mausoleum is a combined B & R created to symbolize both names. But none of this local history explains the stains which Courtnee pointed out looked like actual bloodstains (it wasn't rust). She was right. At the time I denied it out of fear of freaking her and the rest of the family out. But it did look like dried blood and I have no explanation for it.

If you would like to see this bizarre evidence for yourself, you can. We recently unearthed the footage and produced a short featurette on this brief portion of our investigation (less than three minutes long). It's now available for viewing on our channel at: www.ghosthunter.ws entitled: *The Blood on The Crypt.*

A funny side note to this extremely short video. I recently had a fan complain that there was no paranormal activity in this *three minute clip.* Some people just don't get it, no matter how slowly you explain it.

In any case, we climbed the hill into the main section of the cemetery. We felt strangely drawn to a mausoleum overgrown with vegetation that sat off to our left. When we approached it we noticed something quite distressing; several of the niches in the structure had been broken into and the remains were gone. Just then our *Ghost Radar* app started to blip. Signals were coming in from all around us. I then switched on my *Ghost Speaker* app and a word came through that was actually a number, the number *Eleven.* What was the big deal about the word *Eleven?* When we looked up the name on the Mausoleum was *Eleveen.* It was overwhelming.

If this evidence doesn't completely floor you, then quite frankly nothing will. For starters, the odds of the word *Eleven* coming up at random is more than *one in two thousand,* but the odds of that word coming up to match a name on a grave is literally beyond calculation. Since the spirit's family name wouldn't be part of the word bank, the ghost did the next best thing, *it chose the closest possible word.*

It's just logical to assume that this app worked as advertised and actually made contact with a ghost who wanted us to know, beyond the shadow of a doubt that the *Eleveen* family was standing guard. But it didn't end there, we asked why the niches were broken and the remains missing. The next word that came up was, *"Witchcraft."* ... That's a wrap folks!

From The Other Side With Love

This investigation is a good example of a location that has probably never been investigated before. *"Steele Creek Church Cemetery"* is large and very old. In fact, it is one of the oldest cemeteries in the south dating back to the early 1700's. We visited this place on Mother's Day, which we thought may actually act as a catalyst for activity. Also interesting to note that in locations like these, activity normally happens very fast (which in this case, it did). Whether it is blips on the Ghost Radar, EVP, communication on the GMP, or all three simultaneously.

Sadly, Nicky G. was off with her friends doing teenager things that day. So it was only Renee, Courtnee, and myself on this one.

The episode started out calmly enough. We toured the extensive grounds as I pointed out points of interest. Apparently at her age, Courtnee was unaware that there were actually bodies in the above ground tombs. When I made her aware of this fact, the look on her face was priceless and is one of the first things evident on the video.

Once we found a good spot to start working, Courtnee began to conduct a masterful GMP communication. The wind suddenly kicked up at that time which I assumed could be an ADC. It's another one of those things that sounds outlandish to the uninitiated. But winds blowing in response to those looking for signs from beyond, is something that has been experienced time and time again throughout the centuries.

Meanwhile, Courtnee was happily conversing with a spirit named Matilda who was with her family in spirit. This was all learned through the process of elimination via *yes or no* questioning. We wished her a *Happy Mother's Day* which I think everyone involved appreciated. Often times, it seems spirits are looking to communicate and it's rare for a team such as ours to enter in and offer them an audience.

After that session, Renee researched the stones as I remarked at how young most of the people were when they passed on two hundred years ago simply by looking at the death dates in the oldest part of the cemetery. It seemed that if you made it past your 50's you were very lucky. One more reason why I have always believed that older cemeteries are more active than newer ones. But we'll talk more about that in a later chapter.

The only issue I had with this location was the fact that it was smack-dab in the middle of a flight path going to and from Charlotte International Airport. The jets flying overhead every five minutes made EVP all but impossible. And we also had to stop the video several times as the noise was so loud, viewers might mistake it for paranormal activity.

It was also during this episode that I thought I saw a *shadow person* in the very back of the cemetery. I debunked this as being a trick of the eyes. The gravestones as well as a large number of monuments were very old, and quite a few had several tones to them due to moss and discoloration as seen in the photo below. So it was quite easy to mistake one of the stones for a person out of the corner of your eye.

Courtnee using her favorite piece of equipment - From The Other Side With Love

Laurelwood 1 & 2

I touched upon this thought in chapter #2, but I am going to do so again to reinforce this important point. Assuming that ghosts are intelligent entities that are fully aware of their surroundings, it must be no surprise when people try to contact them in popular ghost hunting locations such as *Gettysburg Battlefield*. However, in places like *Historic Laurelwood Cemetery* located in *Rock Hill, South Carolina*, it must be a different story entirely. One has to wonder what any roaming ghosts are thinking when a family such as ours visits and actually attempts to talk to them; are they appreciative?, are they

141

annoyed?, or are they like the living where different people just have contrasting personalities and react accordingly?

Laurelwood contains over 11,414 marked grave sites as of this writing. It was so large and ornate that it was like the proverbial carrot on a stick for any ghost hunter. The cemetery also includes a Confederate monument which was quite breathtaking indeed.

During this investigation we captured a record number of incredibly clear EVP. One in particular was a bit unnerving. If you watch the beginning of *Laurelwood Part #1;* as we were initially walking from the van into the heart of the cemetery, you will hear the first EVP caught on our digital recorder which appears to say *"Come Here... Come Here"* But I have to come clean because that's not at all what it said. What it actually said was *"Come Here Courtnee."* Listen and you will hear it clearly. I changed it for the episode so as not to freak her *or anyone else* out. It was the first and only time I ever changed something like that in an episode and falsified paranormal evidence. Sorry about that, it's a dad thing, and I'd do it again.

Unaware of that EVP when it happened, because we weren't listening to it in real time, Courtnee and I walked along for a bit and both heard distinct footsteps coming from a cluster of trees off to our left. It seemed like a good enough lead, so we started off in that direction.

Once we *made camp* so to speak, I set up an EMF pump for the first time ever in an investigation in order to *feed* the entities so that they may be able to communicate more readily and not drain our equipment which was becoming too common an occurrence. What ended up happening was that we started to get *touched* and experience increased chills. Nicky G. and I went back to the van for another piece of equipment, leaving Renee and Courtnee alone. Renee began having all sorts of strange experiences in the few short minutes that we were gone. When I returned, we felt that it was time to break out the GMP and get to the bottom of this activity.

We felt led to one grave in particular which seemed very close to where Courtnee and I heard the footsteps. So we activated our modified EMF detector, switched it into dialogue mode and not surprisingly, the GMP went into communication mode almost immediately. The entity we spoke to implied that it was his grave we were standing at and that he was the one touching us. Then I started asking questions pertaining to why he was here in the first place? When I came to the big philosophical question, *"Are you trapped here on Earth?"* the communication ceased.

Renee having strange experiences while Nicky G. and I were away from the area - Laurelwood

Forbidden communication

One of the most interesting things that we have learned over the course of our investigations is that, certain questions when asked to an entity will almost always terminate any type of communication immediately.

These are usually the big philosophical/metaphysical questions such as, *"Is there a heaven?,"* *"Why are you trapped here?,"* *"Is this your purgatory?"* Or anything remotely close to that line of questioning. Sometimes we get an answer to these queries, but it's very rare indeed.

For the most part, we are denied.

I once spoke to a pastor/ghost hunter and his theory was that *"Maybe they aren't allowed to answer those questions."* I have heard this echoed by the ghost hunting team of John and Debbie Holliday when we were guests on their radio show as mentioned in chapter #2. One psychic medium actually told me that spirits agree not to divulge these mysteries before they are allowed to communicate with us.

If this is your first book on ghost hunting or the paranormal, I know how all of this must sound. But the fact remains, every time we ask a question like the ones listed above, more times than not, the communication stops almost immediately.

It almost seems as if, we as investigators are allowed *just enough* evidence to validate our findings, but never quite enough for conclusive proof. After dozens of investigations this seems to be by design. Again, it's not just us, almost every investigator I know experiences the same frustrating thing.

Revolutionary Shadows

Huck's Defeat or the Battle of Williamson's Plantation was an engagement of the *American Revolutionary War* that occurred in present *York County, South Carolina* on July 12, 1780, and was one of the first battles of the southern campaign to be won by Patriot militia. The park was dotted with old colonial mansions and relics of all kinds.

I really liked this investigation for several reasons. While there were no known haunts here, it was a fantastic opportunity to investigate the *interior* of some old revolutionary war era homes. Quite rare as most accessible haunted locations are normally outdoors. And of course, it was a battlefield. And from our experience, and the experience of others, prime ghost hunting grounds.

The evidence came in fast and furious. Resulting in an investigation that was a pretty full as far as relevant Ghost Speaker and GMP communication was concerned. We also captured some great EVP on this trip. One in particular was noteworthy.

We were investigating the village doctor's manor of the time period, when a resident ghost became fascinated with Courtnee's level of education as she read off names she found on a list in a room filled with old and possibly haunted objects. She was looking for a name that matched one that came up on the Ghost Speaker to see if we could make a connection. The EVP, spoken clearly as though another flesh and blood person was in the room with us said, *"Can you read?"*

After we left the mansion we went to the actual site of the battle where we commenced with our obligatory GMP communication. Sometimes the spirits are friendly and glad to see us. Other times, they aren't; I'll just leave it at that.

Footsteps Of Antietam

Aside from *Gettysburg, Antietam* was the bloodiest battle of the *American Civil War*. So it's no wonder that paranormal activity is so common on these grounds. We collected a ton of evidence including an EVP stating the name of someone by the name of *"Paul Lee"* whom an apparently trapped spirit on *Bloody Lane Trail* wanted us to contact for some reason. There was certainly *unfinished business here*, but to this day, we can't make heads or tails of it. I researched the name but came up empty several times. We also heard the famous *phantom gun fire* while on our way to *Mumma Cemetery,* which is a common phenomena in the fields.

But the most compelling evidence in my opinion was the clear unmistakable human footsteps we all personally heard walk across the floor of the *Old Drunker Church* where bodies of fallen soldiers were literally heaped in piles near the front door.

There is a saying in the show-biz industry when actors play on old stages where the stars of the past have performed. They say, *"You can feel the ghosts on the floorboards,"* whether or not that is true, is hard to say. But there is no doubt that this is a literal fact in Antietam. The audio (AVP) of those footsteps was captured on our video camera and is available for you to hear in this episode. I find myself playing it over and over again, it's just that amazing.

We also got some insanely relevant words on the Ghost Speaker referring to cannon balls in the field outside of the church. Normally that would have excited me to no end, but nothing could possibly match the sound of those spectral footsteps.

Nicky G. and Courtnee analyzing the energy signatures in the room just after the phantom footsteps were heard walking across this very floor - Footsteps Of Antietam

8

The Palace Twenty Years Later

Paranormal Dream Team... Pictured from left to right: Lance Philip (EKG), Virgil Colligan (ECRIPT), Bobby J. Gallo (G.F.G.H), Courtnee Gallo (G.F.G.H), Officer Shawn Bates (PSY-GUYS), Nicky G. Gallo (G.F.G.H), and Renee Gallo (G.F.G.H) on Camera - Back To The Haunted Palace - Part 1 - The Fountain Of Mystery

Back To The Haunted Palace - Part 1 - The Fountain Of Mystery

W e traveled back to New Jersey, the state the four of us were born for our annual visit back home. We had heard that the old *Palace Theater in Netcong NJ* had been renovated into a children's theater. Millions of dollars were being invested to restore the classic structure. However, upon speaking to the present owner Mr. Steve Fredericks, it was still as haunted as ever. So when I mentioned that I was the decedent of those who built the theater an immediate bond was struck between us. Then when I had asked about doing an investigation, he didn't hesitate for a moment and agreed. After all, with the experiences he was having there such as apparitions, strange sounds, the works; he was eager to get answers as well.

We scheduled a night investigation to find out if Malcolm and Jenny, the famous spirits said to haunt the theater, were still around. To say I was excited was an understatement. Here I was, back in the same place where I started paranormal investigation 20 years earlier. Only this time, I was with my family dream team. Frankly, given it's history, it's reputation for hauntings, and it's sheer size, I really can't think of a better place for a paranormal investigation, and we would not be disappointed.

On this investigation I asked a good friend and paranormal investigator to join us, Lance Philip from *East Koast Ghost (EKG)* and an associate of his, Virgil Colligan from *Ecrypt (East Coast Research, Investigation, and Development Team)*. Lance and Virgil are seasoned investigators who take a very scientific approach to ghost hunting, which was a great balance to the way we investigate which has always been on a more *intuitive* level. Also joining us was my cousin Shawn

Bates who now, 20 years later, was *Police Officer Shawn Bates*. His presence was beneficial for more than nostalgic reasons, he lent an air of authenticity to the investigation. Especially when one stops to consider his training and detective skills. Much like my social media friend Steve DiSchiavi, star of the *Dead Files*. The owner gave us free reign of the theater, even allowing us to lock up after it was concluded.

I hadn't even had the chance to unpack my gear when the activity started. Almost immediately, team members began to hear footsteps in the upstairs balcony. This area of the theater has always been one of the most active hot-spots of the building, where apparitions have been sighted on more than one occasion. You may even remember reading in Chapter #4 about poltergeist activity years ago when a previous owner allegedly had a *bread toaster* thrown at him while he stood in the main area of the theater.

We temporarily held off on climbing the stairway to the balcony and instead gathered in the middle of the ground floor seating area of the theater when suddenly our EMF detector went off with a simultaneous temperature drop captured on Lance's state-of-the-art *Mel-Meter*. This was followed by a collective feeling of chills, and Virgil having actual physical contact with the possible entity causing this activity. The temperature continued to fluctuate in that one area while Courtnee was reading a red anomaly on the Ghost Radar which appeared to be standing right beside us, red is the strongest possible signal.

When the anomalies ceased, we met up with Officer Bates who informed us that he was hearing disembodied voices near the old drinking fountain in the lobby area of the theater. This was then confirmed by Lance who heard them as well. When we approached the area, the fountain became the primary focus at this point in the investigation once we began to get strange EMF fluctuations near the old tile basin. Then just as it had happened in the basement of the Masonic Lodge in Asheville NC, the GMP started to react on command.

We then incorporated a second EMF detector that also reacted when we asked the spirit to come towards it. At first we were stunned, but later attributed the spikes to power lines running through the wall in the back of the fountain. However, that debunk still didn't explain how the GMP was reacting on command when I was holding it. Nor did it explain the EVP that we caught at that exact time which literally spoke Lance's name.

But the crowning moment of this first part of the investigation was when Lance saw an energy orb with his own eyes. Excitedly, I asked him where he saw it. When he pointed to the Men's restroom, without hesitation, I turned and took a picture with my *Bell+Howell S7 Slim digital camera*, and captured it. It was a bright, glowing orb that gave off it's own light, about the size of a large marble.

My conclusions of this experience; that orb was in a precise area opposite the fountain just on the other side of the wall. Yes, the power lines were definitely giving off EMF, but were they being manipulated by this orb as means of communication, thus being able to ping the EMF detectors on command? Perhaps that is why we were drawn to that area in the first place? Which brings us to this vexing question. If ghosts are electromagnetic in nature, does that also mean that they can manipulate existing EMF as well?

All of this activity would have been enough for any ghost hunter or paranormal investigator in a single night, but we were just getting started.

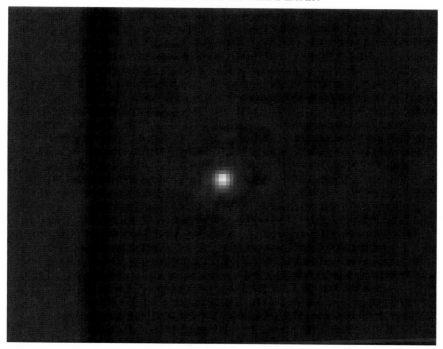

Here it is... The actual orb, seen by Lance Philip and caught on camera behind the Fountain Of Mystery in the old Palace Theater.

Back To The Haunted Palace Part 2 - The Stairway

We headed to the very top *Club Room* above the balcony section of the theater. This was the same room I investigated with the PSY-GUYS 20 years earlier. The site of the haunted piano which we learned, much to our dismay, had been removed and trashed when the theater was renovated.

The first thing Nicky G. did was conduct an EVP session while Renee was filming in infrared. Immediately we noticed that the orb Lance had spotted on the ground floor seemed to be following us and appeared on the footage. Yes, I have no way of knowing for sure if this was the exact same orb, but this is how my deductive reasoning works; I take all of the pieces we find and fit them into a completed puzzle, so that in the end I have a tapestry of evidence that makes perfect sense. Or as much sense as can be expected given what we do.

Nicky G. was getting activity on the Ghost Speaker when it seemed an old friend spoke to me whom wasn't expecting, *Lou Batson*.

Lou worked as the projection operator at The Palace for many years, and knew more about it's history than virtually any man alive at the time. I would spend hours speaking to him in his garage just up the street from the theater. He was a gold-mine of stories and information. He even had some incredible tales of my very own Grandfather and his night-club called *The Wigwam*... But that's a story for another day.

Lou had passed on by the time we went back to the theater for our follow-up investigation. So on a hunch, we turned on our EVP recorder and tried to talk to Lou. As soon as Renee said, *"Hi Lou"* We got an EVP back that said, *"Hi Bob"* This was followed by several team members hearing someone whistling back in the main seating part of the theater.

Nicky G. conducting an expert EVP session in the Club Room of the Palace Theater when the apparent spirit of an old friend came through the digital recorder.

We all marched back down to the floor area again when our orb friend made yet another appearance, this time Virgil took the picture. In it, the orb was actually casting a reflection on the floor!

Renee then went off with the video camera towards the stairs leading back to the balcony. Lance had put an illuminated motion sensor on the steps which went off as Renee was approaching. It seemed that whatever the entity was, it was moving away from her and possibly back up the stairs, so she followed. Suddenly Renee heard a noise off to her left. As she turned, she caught yet another orb in infrared video at that very spot. This one looked different than our other friend but perhaps that's how it looked in this spectrum of light, there really is

155

no way to know for sure.

The activity kept getting better and better. As Renee and Lance descended the stairs back to the lobby, they were unaware of not one, but two orbs floating across the stairway. The best part of this situation was, not only did we catch them on video, but Courtnee saw them with her own eyes and immediately stated so on camera.

Lance followed this activity with an *Ovilus* session back in the main area of the theater. The Ovilus is a stand-alone device created by *Digital Dowsing* that functions similar to The Ghost Speaker. The responses were incredibly relevant, and as he was conducting the session, noises were being heard as well as spirit lights and dark shadows seen coming from the lobby area. His relevant line of questioning seemed to be stirring up energy in the theater.

At this time Renee when was still filming in IR (infrared), when an orb shot straight towards her which she saw through the video camera eyepiece, she was quite startled. We captured it on tape and upon examination, it appeared to have a *tail* which is common for orbs that move at very high speeds.

Courtnee describing the orbs she just saw with her own eyes dancing on the stairway - Back To The Haunted Palace Part 2 - The Stairway

Back To The Haunted Palace Part 3 - Malcolm Finally Speaks

During all of this, the question lingered, were these anomalies related to Malcolm and Jenny? The two enigmatic ghosts associated with this theater for decades? We were about to get that answer.

We pulled out all the stops by straight-up asking the entities to appear for us. The activity seemed to be slowing down dramatically, and that was to be expected. We had generated so much activity up to this point that any spirits who were communicating with us through the many methods we employed, may have expended what little energy they had. So we took out our trusty GMP and tried one more time and it worked. At first the GMP was making a very strange noise that we weren't familiar with in all of the time we had been using it. I offered our flashlight batteries as energy, but instead, I think the entity used my personal aura instead as I got a distinct chill throughout my entire body and simultaneously saw a flash of light just as the GMP made contact. The entity confirmed that it was Malcolm and that Jenny was still with him, but the communication ended almost as soon as it began. As I said, by this point they seemed to be very weak.

It was the chain of events that lent validation to this particular communication. The GMP was making an uncharacteristically odd noise, I saw a mysterious flash of light, I got a chill (possible temperature drop) followed by the GMP triggering into communication mode. For those keeping count, that's four strings of evidence.

Since the entity identified himself as Malcolm, we proceeded back up to the balcony where he and Jenny presumably used to sit and watch the movies during life. We broke out the Ghost Touch device and asked one of them to touch it. Up to that point we had already gotten as much evidence as we needed from this investigation, but this would be icing on the cake so to speak; because just then we captured two incredible Class-A EVP so relevant, they cannot be denied. It was a man's voice asking, *"Can You Touch It?"* Followed by the same voice saying *"Touch it, Ok?,"* Referring of course, to the Ghost Touch device.

It looked like the ghosts wanted to communicate but possibly didn't know how despite my theories on *Universal Intelligence* and the *Morphic Field*. But even that stands to reason. We have had EVP in the past that asked *"How?"* in response to a question we posed to them. So perhaps certain dynamics in the afterlife are more like being alive than we have previously imagined. Some learn quickly while others have an entirely different learning curve.

I switched gears here and asked the spirit of Lou to touch the device. What happened next was interesting. Odd sounds began coming from the old projection booth where Lou spent countless hours as the theater projectionist, but nothing on the Ghost Touch.

We decided to go around the corner to the theater offices located just across the hall from the balcony. Just as we were making our way through the darkness, not one, but two orbs were caught on infrared video. This makes perfect sense from a logical standpoint. The EVP we caught was clearly a man's voice (Malcolm) speaking to someone else (Jenny). So there were probably two entities. Now two orbs show up in the video just after that session, see how all of this fits together? Also interesting to note that these orbs looked *exactly* like the ones caught on the stairway in the previous episode.

In the office area, EVP came in hot and heavy. One said, *"Renee,"* followed by a seemingly female voice saying, *"The Green Room"* (a reference to the old theater days?) and then the pièce de résistance, an EVP of a man saying, *"Yea Jenny"* (Boom Shaka Laka!) Then just like previous times, Renee asked the spirits to approach the EMF detector, and it reacted wildly, except this time, it would not stop. Then as Lance and Virgil entered the room we got an EVP that said *"They're back."* All of a sudden, the EMF left as quickly as it came. The high levels we were getting in that one particular spot ceased without us moving the detector an inch. In fact, that was the end of all activity, period.

Side Notes: To date, this investigation remains one of the most popular episodes we have ever produced with close to *twenty thousand views* on Dailymotion alone. And if you ever attend a live performance at the *Growing Stage Children's Theater of New Jersey*, be sure to look for two things... The first being a brick inscribed with our names inlaid into the front walkway of the theater which we donated as a thank you for allowing us to investigate this historic haunted landmark. The second is in the back of the theater's show program. There you will see a dedication to Malcolm and Jenny. Yes, I'm serious.

Renee testing the camera before heading into the investigation with a full moon in the night sky - Back To The Haunted Palace Theater

9

Things Begin To Get Heavy

For reasons I just can't seem to put my finger on, the Palace Theater investigation which marked the end of season two, seemed to be a turning point for us. The investigations seemed to get more involved, intense, and emotional. We found ourselves, no longer being influenced by the popular paranormal television shows. In fact, at this point, we hardly ever watched them. They were quality shows to be sure, but they didn't even compare to what we were experiencing on every outing. The new dramatic nature the show was morphing into was not by design, it just happened.

This period also began an unexpected metamorphosis. Renee, who usually remained behind the camera, suddenly became the undisputed star of the series, and for good reason. I purchased a set of home-made dowsing rods online, which Renee immediately began using like she had been practicing with them her entire life. She wasn't just good, she was extraordinary. So much so, that experts from around the world who examined our videos remarked how they had never seen someone so gifted with the rods. She was a natural in every sense of the word. Her hands and arms would remain completely motionless, yet the rods responded immediately to every question asked. In fact, she became so good at communicating with these instruments, that I trusted them more than our most expensive equipment. It was a wonder to behold, and trust me, I am not overselling this.

At this time we were also receiving support from fans. One such person, Mollie Abramitis, a seasoned paranormal investigator who watched our show, actually sent us a large box (with a return address from Warner Brothers) containing some of the best possible pieces of paranormal gear, such as a *ZOOM Digital Recorder and Tri-Field Natural EMF Detector.* The best of the best.

Ghosts Of Elmwood

Times Past Haunted Farm

Once we returned to the south, we received an invitation to investigate a haunted farmhouse called *Times Past Haunted Farm* which had a reputation for *shadow people* among other phenomena. The barn in particular had a nasty reputation for being haunted. Especially in the rear where an entity, whatever it was, growled at intruders.

Upon visiting this location, the owner Rose, was more than happy to take us on a tour. Also joining us on this investigation was Jane Horton Starr, an experienced paranormal investigator from a local group.

After hearing the history of the location, we went to the barn where we found what appeared to be a portal or vortex of sorts near the entrance. The temperature in that spot was noticeably colder than the rest of the barn. Before long, despite the fact that it was an 80 degree summer evening in the Carolina's, we were literally freezing in the barn. So much so that we could actually see our breath.

When we attempted communication, we heard a loud bang on the steel roof directly above our heads which startled us all. This actually happened several times during the course of the investigation. Courtnee walked directly into what we suspected was the location of the vortex and got touched on the arm. The photographic evidence was impressive as well. With a large ectoplasm cloud appearing in one of the shots near the location of the growling sound (AVP) which Nicky G. heard herself.

Nicky G. at the exact moment we both heard the voice of a spectral woman calling out to us from this field. - Times Past Haunted Farm

My personal favorite was the EVP we captured during our session. When I asked the spirit to speak into the little red recorder light it responded , *"No, don't like talking"* Later in response to Courtnee asking questions, we would get another incredibly clear EVP saying, *"Little child."* Once again, uncanny relevance.

When we left the barn and ventured toward an allegedly haunted field, Courtnee saw an orb travelling across the landscape (she had developed a knack for seeing orbs). It was the site of a Revolutionary War soldier apparition who was said to appear there every now and again. Since the night had an incredibly bright full moon, I thought that maybe we could capture him on video, but that didn't happen. Instead, Nicky G. and I capped off the night with an unexpected experience. We both heard a distinct female voice calling out to us from the same field, you can barely hear it on the video, but it's there.

Massive ectoplasm cloud shot in infrared at rear of the haunted barn where growling was heard - Times Past Haunted Farm

The Gate Keeper

An *emapth* is a person with *the paranormal ability to apprehend the mental or emotional state of another individual.* The larger question when it comes to the subject matter discussed in this book, is whether or not these same people can use this talent when it comes to those who have passed on? It seems that we were to learn the answer to this

166

query during this particular investigation.

Nicky G. who remained more reserved than the rest of us in past episodes began hitting her stride and increasing her presence on the show. She was exhibiting empathic abilities that were growing sharper with each investigation. This episode is a great example.

However, of all the investigations we have shot to date, this is one I wouldn't do over again. Not since our first investigation in *Old Unity Cemetery* have we felt so unwanted in a location. First off, we experienced massive battery drain. But the troubling part was when Nicky G. who was the clear focal point of the investigation, began to feel extremely oppressed in this relatively old Baptist cemetery. Watch the episode, she's not faking it. It was then that I thought it best to leave. Truth be told, we all felt it to a greater or lesser degree.

So naturally, once we left, we came back two months later because we can't take a hint. This was also the episode where Renee began using the rods to communicate, like I said she was brilliant.

Once again we experienced complete battery drain on our main camera, but now with the help of Renee's talent and the divining rods, we received a clear communication from a spirit who confirmed that it was the one draining our equipment. It also emphatically said (again through the rods) that it wanted us to leave in no uncertain terms. We also got a very clear EVP which said *"Gate Keeper."*

As we were leaving, I took a shot of the gates where we captured a huge, albeit faint, orb. That along with the EVP became the justification for the title of this episode.

Here is the kicker, when I did post-investigation research on the cemetery, I found old newspaper articles from the area that reported a grim story of *voodoo rituals* being performed there. Apparently dead chickens and other paraphernalia were found on the grounds. So one can only guess what happened during that time, and why guardian spirits are now keeping watch by actively influencing visitors with questionable motives to leave. Personally, I can see how a group of ghost hunters who come into a cemetery with strange equipment and start asking to speak to the dead could fit this bill in their incorporeal eyes. This is why, when you get that negative vibe, you need to listen to it.

However, there was a positive note to all of this in the *investigative ghost hunting sense*. The new found knowledge of the cemetery's desecration completely validated the response to the question Renee asked in the episode concerning whether or not the spirit was concerned that we were going to harm the graves.

Also, despite the darker nature of this investigation, we learned a great deal. Nicky G. showed her innate talent as an empathic investigator, and Renee introduced her stunning work with the Rods. Still, we're never going back; it took two times, but we finally got the hint.

Courtnee and Renee upon realizing we had complete battery drain - The Gate Keeper

Thoughts on cemetery investigation

As the reader can clearly see, we have investigated a lot of cemeteries, both large and small, and do so for many different reasons. For example, they are easily accessible (except at night), they are historic, a great deal of emotional energy has been expended in them over the years, and many have reputations for being haunted. To that end, it has always been my contention that *every cemetery is haunted to a greater or lesser degree*. In fact, of all the cemeteries we have ever investigated, there has only been one with no detectable activity whatsoever. And that was the old church cemetery at *Waterloo Village NJ*, which frankly,

169

I found refreshing since it was apparent that all of the souls there were at peace.

Some will say that investigating cemeteries is disrespectful, I disagree entirely. The whole purpose of a cemetery is for the dead to be remembered. Isn't that exactly what we are doing? And in doing so, we give them the opportunity to communicate and resolve any unfinished business they may have. Granted, that's not always easy given the limited modes of communication that we can employ at this present time, but I think it helps.

Fiona Broome's landmark work, *Ghost Hunting In Haunted Cemeteries* is my favorite paranormal book, hands down, and is highly recommended. It's easy to read, has loads of helpful information for the beginning as well as seasoned ghost hunter, and is written with authenticity. I trust what she writes. Which is something I cannot say for every author.

What are the most haunted cemeteries?

As I have already alluded to, cemeteries probably account for the bulk of our ghost hunting. And out of that experience we have come to the conclusion that the older the cemetery, the more likely it is to be haunted. Even in cemeteries that have both older and newer sections, which is common in many places; we have found that activity actually increases the closer we get to an ancient grave site. If you are an active ghost hunter yourself, try this and be the judge.

My personal hypothesis on this is three-fold. The first reason is the historical fact that life was just harder before the age of modern medicine, the electric light, and indoor plumbing. People died much younger than they do in this day and age which can be easily learned by reading dates on ancient tombstones. As I described when discussing the episode *From The Other Side With Love,* It was a blessing to live past your 50's two hundred years ago! That being the case, I imagine there was far more unfinished business in the short lives of those who lived in these eras. And as we have learned again and again, unfinished business accounts for a large number of hauntings.

The second factor is that there is one very important thing that newer cemeteries have that older ones do not... *Visitors!* I am a firm believer that older cemeteries become *active* just by the mere presence of the living. Many spirits *want* to be remembered. In most cases, after grandchildren pass themselves, visits to the family plot become less and less frequent, until they most likely stop all together. Except of course for that person who plants flags on the graves of veterans.

The third and equally important reason is that the dead seem to like to see their earthly resting places cared for. Overgrown, littered, and uncared for grave sites seem to make for increased paranormal activity. Perhaps they are trying to get someones attention to clean things up, fix the stones, or simply mow the lawn!

Finally, there may even be a *fourth* reason, though I cannot take credit for it. A good paranormal investigator friend of mine Kirsten Klang, founder of *Mystical Minnesota Paranormal* actually mentioned something that never occurred to me. We were discussing this subject after a *Facebook Live* Nicky G. and I did recently in a very old churchyard we spotted from the road. I was pointing out my theories when she revealed something that will now change the way I approach old cemeteries going forward.

She then pointed out the fact that many older protestants denominations believe that the soul sleeps in the grave until the day of resurrection (RIP). In metaphysics, it's postulated that we in part create our own afterlife. Put these two beliefs together and you come up with a theory which states that *a good number of spirits may actually haunt their own graves by design!*

I've actually heard a term for this belief called *The Sleep.* Pretty simplistic, but it sums it all up. This dynamic would especially hold true in most cemeteries that date prior to 1900, at least here within the United States, which are for the most part... You guessed it... Protestant.

It's not hard to see the ramifications as well as opportunity available to the ghost hunter if this is true. Vast acres of sleeping spirits residing in many different locations around the country. But I would caution any would-be investigator reading this to approach these locations with the utmost respect and care. If this is reality, it's certainly something that should not be taken lightly or abused.

After imagining the sheer possibilities of this ground breaking revelation, I floated the idea of spirits willingly haunting their own graves by a well-known authority in the field of metaphysics by the name of Cyrus Kirkpatrick author of *Understanding Life After Death*, and *The Afterlife and Beyond,* who replied; *"Unfortunately, I think it IS possible, and it's why hardcore religious beliefs can be a serious problem for people."*

Nicky G. experiencing the strange emotions of a troubled spirit during a frightening investigation - The Gate Keeper

Flowers For Emma

Elmwood Cemetery in downtown Charlotte NC is easily one of the largest we had ever seen. Even larger than Laurelwood. Acres upon acres of the most breathtaking stones and monuments one could imagine. Thousands upon thousands of graves. Some historic, most not. Races separated into two distinct areas. The rich buried far from the poor. You can almost see the human drama play out just by looking at the placement of the stones and monuments. It was utterly amazing.

So it was no surprise that this turned out to be one of the most active cemeteries we had ever seen due to it's sheer size alone. The odds of wandering ghosts among the tombstones were definitely in our favor. Ultimately, the evidence collection turned out to be so extensive, that we had to split the investigation up into three episodes just to keep our audience from experiencing paranormal overload and turning off whatever episode they were viewing before completion. Which would be a bad thing for our audience engagement metric on the video platforms.

Renee again took the forefront with the rods which just came alive in her hands. She and whoever/whatever it was pointing the rods, eventually led us to a beautiful mausoleum with the entities confirming their existence the entire time through a series of questions answered through the dowsing rods. Then, after some further paranormal detective work, we learned that the spirit's name was Emma, one of those interred in the crypt which appeared to be that of a very wealthy family.

Emma's energy was nearly non-existent in the EMF sense, barely reading 0.1 milligauss on our Tri-Field EMF detector, but she was easily communicating with Renee through the rods. Whenever Renee would get a response to a question, not only did the rods move, but the needle on the Tri-Field detector moved ever so slightly, indicating a small energy surge.

Emma departed this life at the young age of 49, and unlike our last episode, we felt perfectly at ease in her presence. She seemed to appreciate the fact that she had visitors. When we asked if she would like flowers in the empty stone plant vases at the foot of the mausoleum, she answered *"Yes."* We broke off communication soon after that, Renee was emotionally exhausted and the needle on our Tri-Field EMF detector when back down to zero.

Renee expertly working the rods - Flowers For Emma

Ghosts Of Elmwood

This particular episode is probably one of the most evidence packed of them all. Truly incredible EVP, expert ghost dowsing, unearthly moaning (this was chilling, but oh so cool), and cutting-edge ghost-box communication. Everything but an apparition, and that was most likely due to the fact that it was a daytime investigation rather than an evening one. In fact, the only daytime apparition I have ever heard about caught on camera is the famous *"White Lady of Bachelor's Grove Cemetery"* in Cook County Illinois.

The highlight of this investigation was our visit to the *Latta Mausoleum*. We had no idea if these was the same Latta family who owned the famous haunted plantation, but it was worth a shot. As fate would have it, it turned out to be a very active location. As we approached, and Renee attempted communication, we immediately captured two astounding and relevant Class-A EVP. First a male, then a female voice; apparently speaking to each other, wondering why Renee was attempting to communicate, and who this woman was. *"Do you know who she is?"* followed by *"No."*

Two spirits together like this is a rather rare occurrence. While we feel that we had two together at the Palace Theater investigation in Netcong NJ, the evidence still stopped short of actually hearing the two of them in a conversation like the one we apparently caught here.

Then when we read off names of the interred in the hopes that one of them was the spirit who spoke into the recorder. The rods remained motionless up until the time I read the name Acton. Suddenly, they sprang to life with a resounding *"Yes."* At the time neither of us knew what gender the name Acton was. When we questioned the spirit with the rods, it indicated that it was female. To confirm and validate this evidence, I did some post-investigation research and came up with the answer. Cemetery records indicated that the full name of the person interred in the mausoleum was *Jane Acton Latta Porcher.*

Like Emma, Acton seemed happy for the opportunity to chat with us. It seemed quite evident that southern charm and grace persist, even beyond the grave. She agreed to allow us to communicate through electronic means as well. In retrospect, this was a mistake. Renee's awe-inspiring use of the dowsing rods was so accurate and flawless, that we could have gotten many more answers if we just continued with the session. But we weren't just interested in communicating, we were also trying to see what equipment worked and what did not.

Then it happened yet again; as with so many other investigations, the first piece of electronic equipment was DOA. Yup, you guessed it, battery drain. Looks like Acton needed some juice in order to keep up the communication. So we detached our dead *Altec Lansing puck speaker* and just used the speaker on the phone instead which wasn't nearly as loud, but it would have to do. This was an app called *Spiritvox SV1,* and was designed by my good friend Danny Roberge of *Big Beard Studios.* A paranormal investigator himself, Danny designed this app with real investigations in mind and not as a novelty or toy.

Our field test of the app with a ghost actually present was a resounding success. But it seemed other spirits were trying to get in on the action as we were now getting male voices and what seemed to be pleas for help. Our suspicions proved to be correct. Arming herself with the Rods once again, Renee found out that the second spirit(s) was not Acton and not part of the Latta clan.

Shorty after that, as we hiked through acres of gravestones we recorded unearthly moaning (EVP) that sounded like something directly out a ghost movie or Halloween soundtrack. The evidence was piling up high, but sometimes you never realize it until you get home to do evidence review. When you are in the moment, time stops and you are just looking forward to the next active event.

This part of the investigation ended with several names coming through the Ghost Speaker app which upon research, helped to piece together the name, *Mary Elizabeth Randall.* We found her listed in the Elmwood records which, once again, proved the validity of the Ghost Speaker. But unfortunately, the records also indicated that the exact date of her death was unknown as well as where she was interred. More than enough reason for a spirit to be at unrest. But the weather turned and it started to rain so we headed out. However, we knew that we needed to return in order to solve this mystery.

Bobby J. heading in the direction of the ghostly wailing - Ghosts Of Elmwood

The Search For Mary Elizabeth Randall

We came back some time later to search for Mary's grave even though it was about a dozen episodes later (we got sidetracked). But I am placing the episode synopsis here because it makes the most sense since I think the reader probably wants to know what happened.

Long story short, we didn't find her grave, but upon reviewing the tape I may have realized the problem which in retrospect, I am kicking myself for. During the communication Q&A, we kept asking about *Mary Elizabeth Russell*, wrong surname, Ghost Hunter fail.

Nicky G. joined us on this one and not too long into the investigation she got her typical accurate vibes leading us in a specific direction where we met the spirit of Annie. Though our communication session kept getting interrupted by strange noises coming from a number of graves nestled in a cluster of overgrown trees (much like Laurelwood). When we approached the location the noises ceased. At the time I debunked this as being a squirrel... Though I never saw the squirrel... Just saying.

Once again we attempted to communicate with Mary Elizabeth Randall. This time using her right name. We began to get some direction, but the longer the session took, the weaker the responses, until the rods just stopped responding altogether.

Courtnee attempting to trace energies in an attempt to find the name of Mary Elizabeth Randall on one of the tombs. - The Search For Mary Elizabeth Randall

No Spirits Allowed

Nicky G. once again took center stage in this premium episode to show what a truly phenomenal ghost hunter and empathic communicator she was developing into.

Upon returning to this staggeringly large city of the dead, we first delivered the promised flowers to Emma's grave (see picture below). If descendants of the family interred in this mausoleum ever did come to visit, I could only imagine their surprise and wonder at the site of fresh flowers in the pots. If only they knew. We also decided to bring flowers to Acton Latta as well.

Nicky G. conducted a very good EVP session, after which we visited the site of the unearthly moaning which we recorded on video in the previous investigation. There we captured a fuzzy EVP which apparently said, *"Really Hurt."*

Nicky G. and I then headed up the hill to an older section of the cemetery as Renee and Courtnee wandered off in a different direction entirely. As soon as my wife and little blonde ghost magnet disappeared out of sight, the Ghost Radar began to light up like a Christmas tree. Words and anomaly blips were coming on strong. Nicky G. experienced an intense intuition that was clearly matching locations indicated by the Ghost Radar to head in a certain direction up a small incline and toward a very specific plot, so I followed.

What we were led to was a stately family monument. The plot was disgracefully littered with beer cans, hence the title of the episode, *No Spirits Allowed, Spirits* actually referring to the alcoholic type which should not be enjoyed in a cemetery. To this day, I don't think anyone got the *double entendre.*

We set up an array of equipment including the SV-1 Spirit Vox which we had success with in this cemetery as well as a Static-Pod to detect any low-level electrical movement in the vicinity. Soon after Nicky G. began the session, we began to hear a distinct name coming through the unit, broken up by syllables; the name was *Blackwood.* Then, when I looked up, much to my amazement (you never stop being amazed by validation) the name coming through the app *was an exact match to the name on the monument.* We now knew who was leading us here and the reason was evident. Don't believe it? Watch the episode and see for yourself.

As we ended the SV-1 Spirit Vox session, a loud *"bang"* sounded behind us, we were quite startled. The paranormal activity in the vicinity was undeniable. Finally, we conducted a Ghost Meter Pro session to learn that it was indeed Mr. Blackwood who may have been the patriarch of the family interred here. Apparently he was upset about the beer cans desecrating the family plot (and who wouldn't be?). And though he communicated that he was with family in spirit, he was also earthbound at the same time; he even reiterated that fact by answering in the affirmative *twice* on the GMP.

Nicky G. and I cleaned up the plot just as Renee and Courtnee showed up. Renee found us in the massive cemetery from approximately a quarter of a mile away solely by use of the dowsing rods to point Courtnee and herself in the direction of where we were hiding in the clump of trees (more validation for the rods). Just then Nicky G. pointed out to me that after we had cleaned up the cans, we experienced no further activity on any equipment.

Nicky G. conducting a communication session with a distraught spirit whose grave was desecrated - No Spirits Allowed

The Hidden Grave Of Thomas Sprot

Whenever people ask me to recommend just one episode, it's invariably this one. Much like *"Ghosts of Elmwood,"* it has everything. Only this episode includes the holy grail of paranormal evidence, *a full body apparition.*

I learned of this cemetery after reading about it on the web. Strange mists and lights had been seen emanating out of this small family burial ground which dates back to the American Revolutionary War. The only problem was that it was on private property. So after due diligence, I found out who the owners were and paid them a visit. When I knocked on the door to their stately southern mansion, an elegant woman appeared to whom I introduced myself and explained why we wanted permission to document the burial ground at night. She not only agreed, she related some very important background stories to me. She also explained that the property had been in the family for over 200 years. Thomas Sprot was a hero of the American Revolution and friend to the *Catawba Indian Nation* who inhabited the area two centuries ago. He was buried in the cemetery along with generations of his descendants.

I planned to come back the next day and do a preliminary investigation at dusk just so that I still had some daylight in order to get my bearings. Since the cemetery was well into the woods, I wanted to know how we were going to get there without getting lost in a southern forest at night which could hold all sorts of frightening things, supernatural and otherwise.

When I arrived, I was alone with nothing but two pieces of equipment, The Ghost Meter Pro set on regular EMF mode, and my trusty Bell+Howell S7 Slim digital camera in video mode because I wanted to document everything I could. Even this preliminary investigation. The place was about as creepy as it gets and was surrounded by an old crumbling stone wall with a rusted iron gate easily a century old or more. So with my gear powered up and running, I approached the small entrance to the burial ground.

Suddenly, as I opened the stubborn gate, my hair stood up on end, it was a feeling stronger than any I had ever before experienced, and the GMP went completely berserk. The needle pinned to 5 milligauss and the sound was reacting more like an alarm. I placed the GMP down on the concrete cemetery post beside the gate, backed away, but it would not stop. I had never seen anything like it before or since.

Moreover, I physically could not enter through the gate; it was like something was actively trying to keep me out. I quickly grabbed the GMP from the post and left.

Later on that evening, Renee and I came back with the rods. Once again, the GMP reacted wildly. She asked through the rods if we could enter the cemetery and they responded, *"Yes."* Nightfall was upon us so I switched the video on the Bell+Howell S7 Slim into infrared mode. I could now easily enter the gates, the feeling of dread was suddenly gone. I took some IR photos only to see small glowing orbs similar to the ones we caught at the Palace Theater in Netcong NJ. It was then when I realized that the GMP which was going crazy moments before, suddenly stopped, completely. After a few more questions with the Rods, one asking for permission to investigate the burial ground, which we obtained; we left once more only to return with Nicky G. and Courtnee. The investigation of a lifetime was on.

We came back and set up a myriad of equipment; including a gift of flowers to pay our respects to the Sprot family (past and present) and thank them for the opportunity to conduct this investigation. I placed the Static-Pod at the gates but this time, there was virtually no activity or EMF detected. Whatever was warning us not to enter previously by virtue of the strong energy signals registering on the GMP, had now clearly given us it's permission to enter.

Nicky G. and Courtnee put the GMP into dialogue mode which immediately triggered, no delay whatsoever. After a short Q&A which didn't reveal a whole lot, we searched and located the grave of Thomas Sprot where we placed the flowers. Then Renee opened up a dialogue, this time with the rods. It seemed we were contacting Thomas Sprot himself. Nicky G. was busy taking a myriad of infrared photos while all of this was going on with our trusty Bell+Howell S7 Slim.

When Renee, still in dialogue with Mr. Sprot mentioned my name to the spirit, both of her rods immediately pointed to me in unison, *mind blown*. This was something neither us of had ever witnessed before. It was one of those surreal moments that confirm what you are experiencing is the real deal.

We then asked if the spirit would pose for a picture. The rods said, *"Yes."* So Nicky G. continued taking photo after photo in infrared which began by showing a small energy orb morph into an ectoplasm cloud. It seemed to be forming next to Renee and was invisible to the naked eye (which is precisely why we shoot in infrared). In subsequent photos *you could literally see the energy being siphoned out of her recorder and into the cloud*. Ultimately, this series of events culminated into our most famous photo that we suspect is the full body apparition of Thomas Sprot.

Nicky G. begins to take shots of Renee during her EVP session...

Unknown and invisible to Renee, the cloud begins to drain energy from her EVP recorder...

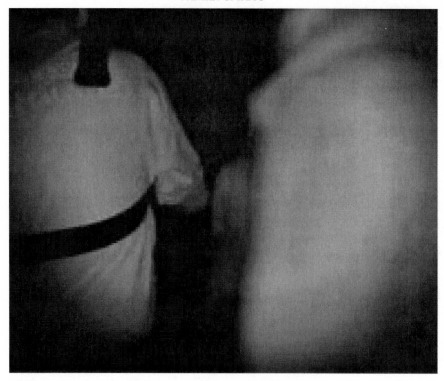

Culminating into what appears to be the full body apparition of Thomas Sprot (on the right) standing next to me, with Renee in the foreground. If you look closely, you can see that the apparition is semi-transparent and that half of Renee's body is visible through the form.

This picture has been examined by many well known personalities in the paranormal field. Reactions have ranged from excitement to utter amazement. But in the interest of complete fairness, I will include this. A very good friend and paranormal colleague of mine, April Abercrombie of *Ghost Advice,* whom I mentioned in the *Unknown Soldiers* synopsis analyzed the photo and pointed out the possibility that this could have been Courtnee moving fast in front of the camera. She was wearing a hooded jacket at the time, and the apparition does appear to have a collar of sorts. So there is that.

On the flip-side, Nicky G. maintains that Courtnee was not in front of the camera when the pic was taken, nor was there any type of bush or headstone in the line of sight; the apparition is semi-transparent. In the original file, if you look closely, you can actually see half of Renee's body through the body of the apparition. Another factor is this, Nicky G. was quite a bit taller than Courtnee at the time; she was holding the camera up chest high as she took the shots. If Courtnee was to walk in front of the camera, only the very top of her shoulders and head would be in the frame. Reviewing the video seems to bear this out. So the angles do seem to play in favor of this not being our little blonde spitfire.

Finally, let's face it, it certainly doesn't look like a little girl. Yea, I know that's not very scientific, but it is intuitive. Even Courtnee who recently viewed this episode again for the first time in about seven years looked at the image and shook her head saying that there is no way it could have been her in the shot.

The session began to die down after that (pun intended). It always seems that the spirits lose the energy necessary to stick around after communicating for any length of time. And of course, if this actually was the full body apparition of Mr. Sprot, then it must have taken an incredible amount of energy and effort on his part to accommodate us in that way. Thank you Mr. Sprot.

Regardless, it was one for the record books. Without a doubt, one of the best investigations ever. And if you ever decide to check out the actual episode, I'm sure you will agree.

Ghost Guide

The midnight investigation wasn't the last we were to see of Mr. Sprot. When Renee and I returned during the day, he apparently led us to the site of the ancient Catawba Indian fort that stood in the vicinity during the Revolutionary War. The reader may think that the term *"led us,"* was merely an assumption on my part, and I can completely understand that. But all one has to do is watch the episode. Something was definitely leading us, and we had double validation on this. Not only were we being led by the dowsing rods, but the GMP on regular EMF mode was actually enabling us to track the EMF signature of the entity through the woods and to the actual site. Both instruments were in perfect harmony and leading us to the same location.

It's another one of those moments where you have to repeat yourself, *"If this isn't enough to convince you, then nothing ever will."*

The most dangerous part of this investigation was dodging the fire ant mounds which were huge and seemed to be nearly everywhere. I had a gut feeling not to bring the kids on this particular ghostly outing and I was right. If anyone was going to get swarmed by fire ants by making one wrong step, it would be me.

The energies finally led us to a very old tree, yup, a tree. I broke out my pendulum and started up a communication. This was the first time (and the last up to this point) that I had used one in an episode. I had trained myself years ago in the art of using this ancient form of divination when I was a full-time performing magician, even though there isn't a trick to it.

Renee standing beside the ancient tree that apparently held great meaning for the Catawba Indian spirits. - Ghost Guide

I seemed to be speaking to an ancient Catawba Indian during this session who gave me information that I had been seeking for quite some time despite any otherworldly directives about forbidden knowledge being relayed to the living . I asked, *"Do you see this area the way it used to be back when it was an actual civilization? Or are you simply haunting the land and seeing it the way it is today?"*

The stunning answer was, *"BOTH."* Which makes sense. Often times ghosts are witnessed performing the same historic ritual over and over again while ignoring onlookers. We often refer to these events as residual haunts. But perhaps in some of these cases we are completely wrong? It's conceivable that some spirits actually want to replay certain moments in their earthly lives over and over. Chalk it up to another one of those great unsolved mysteries. But perhaps we just got a little closer to the truth.

Communicating with an ancient Catawba Indian using one of the oldest methods of spirit communication... The pendulum. - Ghost Guide

Mystery At Blackstock Cemetery

I had read up on an old and supposedly haunted abandoned cemetery hidden in the middle of the woods not far from where we were living in Fort Mill SC, *Blackstock Cemetery* was supposedly a slave cemetery. But I would later debunk that as having no basis whatsoever. It was completely inaccessible in the summer due to vegetation overgrowth, but could be easily found in the winter when the ground was relatively clear.

I soloed this one; which was both exciting and felt strange at the same time. Anything can happen when you are alone in a place like this and some very experienced ghost hunters such as Fiona Broome advise against it.

But being the stubborn adventurous type, I hiked through the woods while sporting a full camera harness and found it. What immediately struck me was the fact that the cemetery was eerily similar to that of the Sprot family plot. Even the surrounding wall was similar. Not surprising really. The two were only several miles apart and most likely used the same construction methods.

When I entered the cemetery the first thing I noticed was that, generally speaking, there wasn't any notable activity despite what I had read on the Internet. I explored a bit, took some shots of the stones, some of which were magnificently carved, and almost stepped into the hole of a grave that had sunken so much, you could literally see down to where the body was buried.

But then I came upon something that was very strange indeed, *an old decaying teddy bear on one of the graves.* This cemetery had been abandoned long ago, and save for some info on the Internet, all but forgotten. So who on earth put this here? It wasn't new, but it couldn't have been very old either. It was just plain weird; especially since it was here of all places and not in a cemetery that was actively visited by the living.

The first impulse of most people would be to pick it up and look at it, or move it to see what is underneath. Some would actually do the unthinkable and take it as a macabre souvenir. But if I have learned one thing in all my time as a ghost hunter it is this; despite the temptation, *you never touch or remove something odd like this.* More times than not, that is the surest way of having an unseen visitor come home with you, and I didn't need that. So instead, I carefully approached the grave with the rotting stuffed animal, and when I got within five feet or thereabouts, my GMP went apoplectic. Needle pinned and an overwhelmingly anxious feeling similar to what I experienced at the Sprot gate came over me. Time to leave... *Fast.*

The mysterious haunted teddy bear of Blackstock Cemetery

Ghosts a' la Mode

This investigation marks our last ghost hunting venture in the south. By this time the family was suffering from mental exhaustion (paranormal hangover) from all of the investigations. But our plans were to move back up north and I assumed that everyone wanted to get in one last adventure in the heart of Dixie. By the way... Never assume.

As fate would have it, I feel that this was one of our least eventful investigations. Maybe it was the fatigue. We were all cranky as well and that just didn't have us on top of our game. Courtnee's bored expressions during the opening monologue are hysterically funny in retrospect as I am waxing on endlessly about the serious nature of the investigation. It's pretty clear that she did not want to be there, and I don't think Nicky G. did either.

We were using a ghost sonar app which picked up EVP rather than EMF and actually worked quite well in a number of cases. Pity that it is no longer available. Which is the downside of many paranormal apps. Once it is no longer updated and supported, you might as well delete it from your device.

We wandered around *Macedonia Presbyterian Cemetery* for a bit looking for any clues we could find. The cemetery was situated just on the other side of a tree line from the much larger town cemetery which I believe was Baptist. I can only assume that the separation was due to a difference in religious belief which was common in the old south. But other than some interesting Ghost Speaker dialogue like *"Shackles & Spear,"* along with a few *African* names coming through which we never experienced before, the evidence, though pretty thematic, was generally low key. We may or may not have had contact with an entity; it wasn't conclusive, and we really weren't *feeling it* so to speak. Though we did get a few EMF spikes in some curious locations. Still, compared to other investigations, it was nothing to write home about. Probably the most interesting thing that happened was the ice cream truck passing by, hence the name of the episode.

Blackstock Cemetery

10

Hometown Spirits

W e were back home at last, at least Renee and I were. The kids spent their formative years in the south but it was time to assimilate to life in New Jersey which I think was culture shock to them. It had been almost two years since our last investigation as a family, and we all wanted to venture back into the mysterious realm of the supernatural.

Though there are easily as many haunts in the north as there are in the south. I stumbled upon one of the most unlikely of places to investigate after getting the lead from a work associate. It was the site of what was, *one of the top ten worst railroad tragedies in US history.* It would turn out to be a very dark investigation.

Tragedy At Rockport

We have been told that the production of this episode was one of our best yet. I don't know about that, but I can tell you that it was probably the first one where I had to do actual historical research beforehand. This was done in order to get the story straight, so that the viewer could understand the indelible impact of what had happened there.

To make a very long story short, back on June 16, 1925, a group of German Americans were on their way back to Germany when the train carrying them derailed during a violent storm, which flooded debris onto a grade crossing, derailing a Lackawanna Railroad DL&W train. The crash killed 42 passengers, five crewmen and injured 23 others. Reports say that one passenger car flipped on top of the steam engine where nearly everyone was burned alive. Horrific to say the least. The area is still littered with burnt railroad ties from that tragedy. Today, a brass plaque affixed to a boulder nestled between a grouping of bushes is the only reminder to visitors of what happened there so many years ago.

This episode once again showed how dead-on accurate an Ovilus or Ghost Speaker type of app can be in the right location. Some of the words that came through were 100% relevant to this tragedy and the time it took place. In this case, I will leave it to you to watch the episode and see exactly what I referring to.

We performed a number of tests during the investigation with moderate results; but when we conducted a SV1 Spirit Vox session, we heard the distinct words, *"we are burning"* along with some other disturbing messages. I really want to think that this is a text book example of a *residual haunting*. The energy that must be soaked into the surrounding countryside certainly does support this theory. I cannot imagine spirits having to relive these events in perpetuity.

The end of the episode did however end on a rather humorous note when something through the Ghost Speaker called me a *"Dork."*

Nicky G. keeping her spirits high during a very dark investigation - Tragedy At Rockport

Witch City Part 1 - Ghost In The Witch House

After the above investigation it was time for a ghost hunting vacation; and what better place than Salem Massachusetts, *The Witch City.* This would prove to be an extremely productive trip both in terms of enjoyment, as well as some really incredible evidence.

I wanted to do this right. So I booked the family suite at the historic *Salem Inn*. I cannot imagine a more appropriate place for a ghost hunting family to stay, as the hotel has a reputation for being exceedingly haunted itself. As soon as you enter the old mansion you can literally feel the energy emanating from the ancient plaster walls. The building allegedly hosts a number of ghosts: *The ghost of a cat, the spirit of a spectral woman who sits by a window in the breakfast area, Captain Nathaniel West the original owner of the structure whose portrait hangs in the parlor, the spirit of a small boy who throws pebbles at patrons, and a woman named Katherine who is said to haunt room 17.*

After checking into our suite, our first stop was right across the street. The famous *Jonathan Corwin House*, also known as *The Witch House*, which was the home of Judge Jonathan Corwin (1640–1718) and is the only structure still standing in the city with direct ties to the Salem witch trials of 1692.

We used a few pieces of ghost hunting gear as we toured the house, such as the Phantom Radar on Nicky G.'s phone and my personal favorite, the Spirit Touch device. During our upstairs investigation of this extremely ancient building, we were attempting to avoid other visitors. One woman in particular, seemed extremely interested in what we were doing. So we did an artful dodge every time she came close. You never know whether people like this are friend or foe of the ghost hunter.

It didn't take long until blips were showing possible entities in the room we were searching. When I activated the Spirit Touch and asked any present entities to touch the yellow detection field (in a very quiet voice), the LED went off. Something definitely resided there, but what made this episode even more worthwhile was the session we did in the courtyard of the Salem Inn after nightfall.

We first enjoyed a real New England lobster roll at a nearby restaurant, before heading back to where we were staying the night. We set up some equipment in the side courtyard of the Salem Inn on an ornate wrought iron table. The area was devoid of any other guests, it was very dark, and seemed to be the perfect venue for our investigation.

Activity began almost immediately, as blips on the Phantom Radar showed an entity standing in our midst. Then the colors began to change on the Static-Pod that we placed on the courtyard table sensing and validating what was being shown on Nicky G.'s app. But the most chilling and spectacular part of this session was when a *spirit actually walked in front of Nicky G.* which was clearly caught on camera. We've never seen anything like it before or since. This may count as our third full body apparition caught on media if you count the shadow person at the *Old Pour House in St. Augustine...* Or not.

Nicky G. tracking ghosts in the Witch House - Witch City Part 1 - Ghost In The Witch House

Witch City Part 2 - Spirit Laughter At Old Burying Point

It can be difficult sleeping in a notably haunted hotel. Every bump and thump seems to be a ghost. But eventually, exhaustion overtakes you and off to *paranormal slumber land* you go.

The next day saw us up bright and early. After a wonderful meal in the haunted breakfast area (no ghost peeking out of the window unfortunately). We headed downtown to investigate the *Old Burying Point*. Along the way, Renee and I had a very strange, almost surreal experience.

We had taken a trip to Salem together before the kids were born. Even staying in room 13 of the *Salem Inn*. And that fact spawned the first weird realization that came to both of our minds simultaneously, *The Salem Inn didn't look the same as it did back then*. We just didn't recognize it, and we have never had that problem before, no matter where we have been.

I would venture to say that the vast majority of people will usually recognize places they have visited at a later date, but this building somehow looked different. It even appeared to be facing in the wrong direction with respect to downtown. After that, while walking up and down the streets, particularly around *Old Burying Point*, we both said the same thing to each other once again. Salem during our previous trip looked absolutely nothing like it did today, not even remotely close. We could not recognize anything. In fact, we actually questioned whether or not we were even in the same city. It almost seemed like an *alternate reality*. I'm not exaggerating in the least when I say that we actually felt shaken and confused by the transformation. Renee even remarked that the famous *House of Seven Gables* looked like it was picked up and moved to a different location, I agreed.

Even now, it seems odd that both of us would have the same *Twilight Zone* type of experience in the same exact way. Regardless, I will just chalk it up to the fact that presently, Salem has simply become a built up city and tourist attraction. Not the charming New England village it once was. Sadly, it's lost much of it's atmosphere and mystique over the years. Yeah, let's go with that.

As we meandered into the business section of Salem, we wandered into a well-known *magick shop* where Nicky G. and Courtnee got readings from a real Salem witch that proved to be quite eye-opening. This was the same psychic who told Courtnee about her personal protection from St. Michael himself! A fact which still blows me away and that I believe for some odd reason to be true. In that same shop, I actually bought a candle with the image on St. Michael on it that now resides in my office. I still think it is strange why pagan witches would use the image of a *Roman Catholic Saint* in any way whatsoever. Maybe next time I'll ask her.

After that unique experience we headed into *Old Burying Point* which boasts to be the second oldest cemetery in the United States. Even hosting a pilgrim from the Mayflower! Though it is a popular attraction and nearly all of the grass has been worn away by the constant footsteps of tourists, it still screams out for ghost hunters to investigate; especially given some of the infamous personalities who are interred here. Pictured below is Courtnee investigating the grave of one of the actual *witch hysteria* trial judges.

This investigation was to provide one of our most unique and creepy EVP. Here is what happened. We were in the rear of the burial ground near a large tree that seemed, over time, to be literally pulling the stones out of the ground. We went back there because frankly, we wanted some privacy in order to investigate. As I already mentioned, that graveyard is a very popular tourist spot. There seemed to be at least several people meandering around at all times, while we were attempting to conduct our investigation.

Massive tree amongst the ancient grave stones at Old Burying Point in Salem Ma. This is the exact spot where spectral laughter was recorded on our video camera.

So upon finding a good spot, and attempting a communication, Courtnee and Nicky G. were delivering some very funny lines that had us all in stitches. While we were joking around on camera, you can hear us all laughing; suddenly, a *fourth* female voice which was on a different frequency all together, and clearly not any one of us, *Begins to laugh with us!* This was caught through the video camera microphone, not the digital recorder. Guess there is a first for everything!

The episode ends with an apparent GMP communication with the specter of Susannah Martin, one of the accused, which we weren't expecting at her memorial which lies just adjacent to *Old Burying Point.* What made this communication important is that all of the questions we asked her have already been documented by historical record. Every single response was historically accurate concerning the witch hysteria of 1692.

Courtnee investigating the grave of one of the original Salem witch trial judges. - Witch City Part 2 - Spirit Laughter At Old Burying Point

Witch City Part 3 - Gallows Hill

If you ever visit Salem and ask where the accused were hung, you will be directed to a public park complete with swing sets and monkey bars. However, this isn't where the travesty happened. Upon questioning locals *who were in the know*, we were directed outside of town to a small fenced in clearing directly behind a drug store. Located in Danvers Mass. with no historical markers of any kind. The area wasn't part of Salem proper as it is zoned today, but it was back in 1692! All of the geography checked out with the history books. The stream where the bodies were carried away after the hangings, and a small stone fence around the area, which served as the border of a slaughter house built on the same location years after the historic events took place in order to *cover up* what had happened on that unholy spot.

Only Nicky G. and myself investigated these grounds. The air was thick with such depressed energy, you could cut it with a knife. The sky was overcast which also lent an air of dreary melancholy to the surroundings. So much so that it can actually be felt by merely watching the footage. The ground was littered with refuse, much like the *Blackwood grave at Elmwood Cemetery in Charlotte NC*. It seemed like people there were in the habit of disrespecting this historically significant area and that is always a recipe for paranormal activity.

The only equipment we used here was the Ghost Meter Pro which did not disappoint. Sometimes when we wanted to get in and out of an area quickly, it's all we needed other than of course, a camera. Today was one of those days. We felt uncomfortable there, but our need to get answers outweighed our reluctance to investigate the area.

Nicky G. began a sweep of the area, and after about three minutes or so, began to get some *off the chart* readings with the GMP in ghost detection mode. It seemed that we caught the attention of someone on the other side of the veil. Which makes sense since this wasn't a tourist spot in any way, shape, or form. The presence of the living was probably a novelty for any spirit wanderers who may reside on that hill. Plus, very few people knew about this area other than those who used this as a drinking spot. And I could only imagine the experiences they have had there.

We continued to search the area for any other clues that may lead us to confirm what we were told about the top of this hill. Once again, the GMP spiked with a very high reading. We switched the GMP into dialogue mode to see if we could contact whatever was making this equipment react so violently. It took awhile but eventually the GMP triggered. Nicky G. then conducted a masterful, and longer than typical communication with a spirit who regularly visits this area.

The first question asked was if the spirit present was one of the witchcraft *accusers*. The reason we asked this first was because sometimes we get skeptics who see our GMP communications and will say that most of the time, the unit pings a *"Yes"* answer by default. Rarely if ever, does it start with a *"No"* response. Again, that is what the skeptic who doubts the validity of this equipment will say. So we wanted to begin by asking a question that would most likely garner a *"No"* response since we doubted any of the accusers of that day had the guts to watch the executions which they knew were caused by their own false accusations. Sure enough, it pinged a *"No."*

Then we asked if the ghost was one of the accused, again a *"No"* response. Was it a spectator to the hangings?, *"No."* The third time in a row, very rare to be honest, but once again speaks to the validity of the GMP.

Then, Nicky G., as though she had an epiphany (or her intuition kicked in), asked if it was a family member, *"Yes."* So I looked at Nicky G. and reiterated the question. All of a sudden a strong *"Yes"* came through again! The ghost was listening to us and double confirming this fact. We asked a few more questions; the spirit apparently came there often and everyone involved was at peace (that's the good part). But my last question, *"Do you just come here just to remember and not forget?,"* got a *"No"* response. Then it left abruptly, apparently there was unfinished business at hand that will forever remain a mystery.

Nicky G. connecting with a spirit at Gallows Hill

Witch City Part 4 - Haunted Room 17

Our final episode in Salem was an interesting one; we saved the best for last so to speak. After all, you don't stay in a famously haunted hotel without investigating it!

I dutifully asked the nice woman at the desk if it was permissible to hang out in the parlor after hours. Not only did she agree, but when she learned who we were, she immediately showed us a section of tile that was imprinted by spirit with the image of a woman! But it gets better. She told us that there was one room in the hotel more haunted than any of the others, and unless people specifically request it, they do not rent it out due to paranormal activity. *Room 17*, said to be haunted by the spirit of Katherine.

Well, you could imagine our excitement which was made even greater when she handed us the key to the room and gave us permission to investigate! A rare opportunity indeed!

Before we went up to the room, we set up our planned parlor investigation. By this time the desk was closed and we were able to set up the works on the coffee table in front of us which included a *Laser Grid* pointing up towards the ceiling. The stern portrait of *Captain Nathaniel West* staring down at us the entire time definitely added to the ambiance.

Looks like Captain Nathaniel West has met his match. One of the world's greatest ghost hunters, doing some pre-investigative work before our night-time blackout - The Parlor

There were many different energies detected in the room. The Static-Pod was especially active and I made doubly sure that we weren't doing anything to stir up that type of energy while we were sitting there. Despite the fact that we were motionless, the pod reacted as though someone was dragging their feet across the rugs.

Another interesting phenomenon came from the large bird cage that resided in the parlor as well. For the most part the birds were silent; then suddenly, without any provocation, they started to squawk as though something was threatening them. Perhaps the birds were reacting to the fabled *ghost cat of the Salem Inn?*

We collected a few more pieces of evidence, then packed up our gear and headed up to room 17. Upon entering, we immediately found it to be at least ten degrees cooler than the rest of the hotel. I checked the thermostat and found that it was turned off, ruling out the air conditioner. We hastily set up our equipment (why "hastily" I have no idea since we had nowhere else to be except in the hotel that night!) including the Laser Grid on the wall to detect any shadow movements, and once again, the Static-Pod which we placed directly on the bed. Nicky G. explaining to the camera where we were and what we were about to attempt. Then almost as soon as Nicky G. was done with her monologue, Courtnee noticed that the pod began reacting much as it did in the parlor.

Nicky G. and Courtnee decided to conduct a GMP session. It searched for energy much longer than usual for a haunted location, but eventually triggered into communication mode. The session was relatively short with no earth shaking information being obtained other than the fact that the spirit admitted that it was the one who haunts the room and is responsible for the mischievous activity that the room was know for; such as pulling the covers off of people during the night.

During this event, we captured several orbs in very relevant and strategic locations. One orb seemed to be travelling at a very high rate of speed, while the other was *literally touching* the Static-Pod which continued to give us a Vegas style light show!

Then, while I was performing a Ghost Speaker session, Renee, who was on camera at the time, saw an orb with her own eyes fly behind Courtnee who was narrating the activity thus far for the camera. Courtnee, though visibly shaken continued her recap of events like a true Para-Celeb. The spirit then recognized that we were on vacation and actually said so through the Ghost Speaker! We then did another GMP session and this time received some very relevant information.

We tried to get the spirit to walk across the Laser Grid but to no avail. I have yet to gather any compelling evidence from this very cool looking piece of equipment. I will keep trying, but it may be one of those *well thought out* theories that doesn't work in actual practice. Because the way I see it, if I truly believe that we are connecting with a ghost at any given time, it's obliging us by answering questions through any of our ITC devices, and giving us EVP; then it's logical to assume that if I ask it to walk across a Laser Grid it probably would. Therefore, it's also logical to surmise that they are probably doing as we ask but the grid is just incapable of detecting their movement. I hope that all made sense.

At the conclusion of that session, as has happened so many other times after we have captured multiple strings of evidence, all activity on our equipment ceased. Nothing on the Static-Pod, Ghost Meter Pro, or Ghost Speaker. Whatever was visiting us seemed to have left.

Note: I am really embarrassed about a *faux pas* that kept rearing it's ugly head during the entire investigation of the Salem Inn. I constantly referred to *Captain Nathaniel West* as *The Colonel* when I should have been referring to him as *The Captain*. I don't usually make these kinds of mistakes, but when I do, I make sure that I do it at least a dozen times like I did here. That is the second time we had the same type of ghost hunter fail and I take full responsibility for it.

Two mysterious orbs during our communication session. One as indicated by the arrow. The other actually touching and making the Static-Pod react. Gee, I never knew dust could do that! -Witch City Part 4 - Haunted Room

17

The Parlor

This short episode opens up with additional footage of our investigation of the *Salem Inn* parlor. We actually released this video selection as a stand-alone featurette on the web where as of this writing, has received almost 13k views on Dailymotion alone.

It's a pretty cool video actually. A chance to see what a *black-out* investigation in a famously haunted hotel looks like. Filmed entirely in infrared, we couldn't see a thing at the time except for the lights on our instruments and the Laser Grid on the ceiling; I really enjoyed this investigation. There is simply nothing like being able to sit on a comfortable antique couch while investigating the supernatural in a stately parlor that offers complimentary sherry as a bonus... Sign me up again please!

However, evidence was indeed captured such as; temperature drops, Tri-Field meter fluctuations on command (I love those), and some interesting experiences including what appeared to be a conversation on our SV-1 Spirit Vox between several ghosts. A spectral party that Nicky G. tried to break up; definitely something worth checking out. After all, thirteen thousand other people have!

Courtnee contacting Sophia - Shades Of The Past

Shades Of The Past

What began as an impromptu investigation, very quickly became one of our most watched episodes with over 11k views to date on Dailymotion alone. But once someone views this investigation, it's easy to see why. This is easily one of the top 10 most active locations we have experienced.

The area was a 200 year old town square with burial ground that wasn't too far from our home in New Jersey at the time. It was another one of those investigations that was just done on a hunch that something might linger there, and we were right. As soon as we approached the abandoned church, first the Ghost Meter Pro, then the Tri-Field EMF detectors sensed energy where there shouldn't be any. At one point, whatever was making the Tri-Field react seemed to be playing a cat and mouse game with me. Every time I would move away, the EMF intensity levels would spike, and vice versa.

We began exploring different parts of the graveyard and were getting strong anomalies on the Ghost Radar along with some fairly relevant words, followed by EMF spikes in very specific locations among the stones. At one point we even got an "AVP" (Audio Voice Phenomenon) when Courtnee actually heard a ghost voice with her own ears, saying *"Yes,"* in response to her question. No Ghost Meter Pro needed!

Spirits in this location seemed very willing to approach our EMF detectors. As we came near one specific grave, the hair on my neck stood up and the Ghost Meter Pro in regular EMF mode reacted strongly. Then Nicky G. obtained a communication which suggested the entity was upset over the cracked headstones. Courtnee immediately followed with a GMP session that lead us to believe the entity's name was Sophia. She answered quite a few questions until I asked the big philosophical one which was whether or not she was trapped in this plane of existence. Guess what happened next? Yes, as expected, communication ceased once again. Then moments later, all of our equipment died.

See the pattern? Communication termination coupled with equipment failure has happened to us in numerous investigations, in locations hundreds of miles apart, and all under very similar circumstances. Coincidence? I think not.

Nicky G. documenting unusual EMF spikes. - Shades Of The Past

Gettysburg Part 1 - Ghosts & Girls In Gettysburg

We have investigated haunts ranging from small forgotten burial grounds, to large haunted structures, but it was time to investigate what has been called the most haunted stretch of land in the world, *The battlefields of Gettysburg.*

To do this right, I enlisted some help in the form of the *Ghost Gals*. A paranormal team that works almost exclusively in the Gettysburg area. They were only too happy to investigate with us, and led the team to some extremely active locations that were far off the beaten path, and where few tourists visited.

This actually turned out to be one of the most enjoyable investigations we have ever been on. It was great to work with another paranormal team to see the differences in the way everyone worked, as well as the similarities.

We met the Ghost Gals at a local gas station, from which they escorted us to a section of Gettysburg called *East Calvary Battlefield*. Apparently they had investigated this area before with great results. Renee and Brigid Mcdermott Goode started the momentum by capturing some incredible Class-A EVP that seemed to echo what the girls were saying. We were only investigating about five minutes before we captured something significant. Gettysburg was truly living up to it's haunted reputation.

It was also Brigid who showed Nicky G. and Courtnee how a pro conducts an EVP session. Though we have had excellent success using our methods, she was showing them how to review EVP in real time. Priceless ghost hunting lessons. And it was wonderful that they were learning from someone other than myself who had credibility in the field of the paranormal.

Brigid Mcdermott Goode of the Ghost Gals giving expert advice to Nicky G. and Courtnee on how to record and listen to EVP in real time.

Then Pamela Spicknall from the Ghost Gals conducted an expert pendulum communication using my very own crystal. It was during this communication that one of the Ghost Gals, Nicole Novelle (Nicky Paraunormal) heard an AVP with her own ears that I was able to verify after evidence review. The answer to one of the questions posed to the ghost through Pamela was *"No."* At that exact moment, not only did Nicole Novelle hear it with her own ears, but it was captured through the video camera mic as an EVP. Stunning evidence.

I still believe that dowsing can be every bit as convincing as what we capture electronically. Since I have a background in pendulum communication, I really appreciated watching Pamela work. She was far better than I. Courtnee even had the chance to partner with Nicole Novelle as they documented peculiar temperature changes in an open field using both a Mel-Meter and our Black&Decker temperature gun which was no small feat.

Courtnee and Bobby J. listening intently during a SV1 Spirit-Vox session -
Gettysburg Part 1 - Ghosts & Girls In Gettysburg

Gettysburg Part 2 - Girls In The Dark

As you probably guessed by the title of this episode, this was our
nighttime investigation with the Ghost Gals. It was both exciting and
productive capturing some great evidence. It is also the best out of
the three Gettysburg episodes in my opinion.

The two teams finished up in *East Calvary Battlefield* after Nicky G.

began to have empathetic feelings towards the ghosts present and was starting to feel melancholy in much the same way as she had during *The Gatekeeper*. So we felt it best to wrap it up at that particular location. We were then brought to another little known part of the battlefield that had very sparse traffic, and the park hours allowed us to investigate a bit after nightfall.

Courtnee and Nicole Novelle discussing the use of the Mel-Meter

When the sun was finally gone, this section of the Gettysburg battlefield took on a whole different atmosphere. Not far into the investigation we were starting to get Static-Pod activity when the

Ghost Gals began to play *trigger music,* as well as intelligent *Echo-Vox* communication which actually said the word *"Ghost."* After which several of us saw a human-like shadow figure amongst the tree line about 30 yards away. So I decided to investigate alone which was both unnerving and exhilarating at the same time. I armed myself with my Bell+Howell S7 Slim and ventured out. It was creepy alright. Here I was in the middle of Gettysburg battlefield alone at night. The rest of the team a substantial distance away. *"Isn't this how most horror movies start?"* I thought to myself, anything could have happened. Sadly, I didn't catch any evidence of a ghost soldier. On the other hand, I wasn't exactly sure what I was going to do if I did.

Towards the end of this investigation, I took some shots of the old cannon that we were camped next to. As a parting gift from beyond, I was allowed to capture one of the best examples of a *spirit orb* to date.

A stunning shot of a civil war era soldier still at his artillery post. At least that's the way I see it - Gettysburg Part 2 - Girls In The Dark

Gettysburg Part 3 - Confederate Ghost Soldier

This last investigation in Gettysburg was interesting for several reasons. Around this time on the social media boards, the classic Ghost Radar app was under fire for allegedly being fraudulent. So we wanted to put it to the test, *I mean really test it.* The results were nothing short of astounding. The app was actually answering questions that I was putting to it in real time and even echoing words that Courtnee spoke!

However, it turned out to be a relatively short investigation as Renee had strong feelings about the location and turned us back when a spirit seemed to be leading us down a certain dirt path. You may also notice a conspicuous absence of Nicky G. in this episode. She was so wiped out from the investigation the night before that she fell asleep in the van, poor thing.

Bobby J. behind the camera - Shades Of The Past

11

Other Episodes

Clinton Road - America's REAL Haunted Highway

What began as a joke, quickly became one of our most watched episodes of all time. Frustrating when this ended up getting more views than many of our other episodes which actually have solid evidence to offer. It was initially taped as a satire of the show to be used solely as a marketing tool to direct viewers from YouTube to Dailymotion; but as fate would have it, it exploded on YouTube with 112k views to date! It's worth checking out just to read the viewer feedback who thought this particular venture was to be taken seriously. Clearly, some people can't take a joke.

The footage merely consisted of a drive down the allegedly haunted *Clinton Road in West Milford NJ* with my mom in the van, yes, my mom, and described what we saw as we made our way down and around the bends in broad daylight. The only interesting thing about the footage were some strange orbs at the end. Still not sure what they were. But it was very funny, and good entertainment if nothing else.

Electromagnetic Ghost Voices - Gallo Family Ghost Gear

Gallo Family Ghost Gear was supposed to be the start of a spin-off series with the intention of testing out new equipment designed for paranormal use. Such videos tend to be mundane at best. Therefore we felt they didn't necessarily fit into the same catalog as a full investigation format.

I soloed this experimental outing at a section of the *Old Morris Canal in Stanhope NJ*. It was about 100 degrees near a stagnant (but allegedly haunted) canal way. I'm not afraid of ghosts, but all of the bugs, ugh! I was investigating an ancient mill that resided along the banks upon the recommendation of a friend using brand new technology by *Digital Dowsing* designed to actually record EMF as an audio signal that could then be played back. The theory was that if ghosts manifested and thus communicated through EMF, then perhaps the energy itself could be interpreted as words. It was a long shot for sure, but worth a try.

The end results were funny buzzing noises when I asked questions to anything or anyone who may be present. Untested tech capturing unusual evidence to say the least. But hey, one paranormal investigator from *The United Kingdom* called the experiment *"Brilliant."* I'll take it!

The Mystery of Cat Swamp Hill

I decided to release this footage as a full blown episode despite the fact that I soloed this due to one piece of evidence that completely blew me away. This was the site of a grisly murder back in the early part of the 20th century. A fellow was hijacked by highwaymen and killed on this spot.

There is nothing to see at this location except a marker describing what had happened there. I had a few pieces of equipment. The GMP, The Ghost Speaker, and of course, a camera. The Ghost Speaker has already been explained as an electronic dictionary of more than two thousand words that theory states, a spirit can choose from in order to communicate. So what are the odds that at the very location where a murder took place, I actually got the word *"Murder"* to come through on the very first try? ... Jaw drop, episode released.

Colonial Whispers

Yes, a strange EVP was caught alright, but it was virtually the same EVP that I caught by the *Old Morris Canal* using the EVP mic. Other than that, I got pretty much nothing. But for those who are really following this, the EVP caught was virtually identical. Perhaps that's how spirits sound when captured through this cutting-edge device? It also captured what appeared to be *creepy echoing footsteps* of some sort; not as exciting as some of our other episodes, but interesting and maybe even a little bit weird.

Ethereal Tour Guide

Another solo investigation filmed while I was on a business trip to New England. I couldn't resist. The cemetery was so old and massive that I just had to do it. Plus it was a chance for me to take my time and test out some new paranormal apps; some worked, some did not. The title came from the fact that the Ghost Radar seemed to be leading me to various tombs for some confusing reason I couldn't fathom.

This may not be the most compelling episode of the lot, but it is worth watching just to see an amazing, two century old New England cemetery with all of those classic old stone carvings. Plus the crab cakes I had nearby were the best!

Spirit Touch ITC Device - Field Test at Gettysburg

If you enjoyed our investigations in Gettysburg with the *Ghost Gals*, then you will love this episode where we pulled older footage on an equipment test and released it as a short featurette. We often did this to promote the larger series. But these episodes are short and get right to the point. Besides, I hate wasting good footage that I think is interesting myself.

Orbs and Ectoplasm in St. Augustine - ICOM Paranormal

Technically our very first episode when we weren't even *Gallo Family Ghost Hunters* yet, just *ICOM Paranormal*. A slideshow compilation of shots taken during the St. Augustine investigations. I still enjoy watching this to see if I can spot any missed anomaly in the photographs.

More videos on www.GhostHunter.ws to binge watch

The reader is probably wondering who is going to watch all of these shorts? Well, you'd be surprised. We have fans that follow everything we do and have actually referenced material from many of these videos in social media forum chats.

- Promo Trailer for Gallo Family Ghost Hunters
- How To Make Your Very Own Ghost Detector
- Ghost Meter Pro Review and Haunted Field Test
- Ghost-O-Meter Android App Cemetery Field Test
- Point of View Ghost Hunt - DVR Sunglasses Field Test
- Ghost Hunter Accepts Ice Bucket Challenge!
- Gallo Family Ghost Hunters Catch-O-Ghost Contest!
- The Blood On The Crypt
- The Scent Of The Dead

See? ... I told you I hate wasting footage! But seriously, also check out our ICOM Paranormal Facebook and Instagram pages for exclusive pics, *even more salvaged footage*, articles, schedules, and live video feeds.

The End... Or is it?

What I learned after doing the few solo investigations you see listed, is that the show just isn't the same without the entire family as a team. Nor do I seem to experience as much activity alone. It's more than apparent that the girls have much better energy when it comes to attracting spirit, and by extension, evidence.

It's our hope to launch this book with a come-back episode. Various locations including *"Sleepy Hollow NY,"* are currently being considered as well as some other lesser known locations with pretty incredible haunted history behind them. If you are affiliated with a paranormal group and would be interested in doing a group investigation and possibly appearing on an episode of Gallo Family Ghost Hunters. Please contact us through our social media pages. We would love to solve some mysteries with you!

12

Conclusion

Is modern science stuck in the past?

I ask this strange question because, after what we have experienced, we know one thing for certain, *You can't put a ghost in a bottle*. Nor would we want to. The *scientific method* where evidence must be peer reviewed and proven beyond a reasonable doubt will never work in this field; at least for the foreseeable future. If this is what people are looking for, they simply need to find a new hobby.

For centuries, Metaphysics has tried to tackle the tough questions of the nature of reality, including those of a spiritual nature. However, despite some very compelling arguments and reasoning; skeptics will continue to scoff at this branch of understanding due to the fact that there is no material basis for it's philosophy. But since ancient times, it's *wisdom,* as well as religious belief, is all we really had to go on.

We must look ahead to new, provable scientific theories such as quantum physics which is making great strides when it comes to explaining how consciousness controls and permeates all things.

One such resource is Dr. Robert Lanza's ground breaking theory of *Biocentrism.*

Research is now being conducted by top quantum physicists, doctors, and scientists who are beginning to prove that consciousness itself may not be housed in the brain at all. Or in some studies, very precise parts of it. Such as research being done by Professor Stuart Hameroff MD at the University of Arizona. A physician anesthesiologist who postulates that consciousness is housed in the *microtubules of the brain.* This potentially ground-breaking discovery may eventually answer the age old question of where the *spirit* is actually housed in the human body while we are breathing.

Other brilliant minds surmise that the brain merely serves to act as a limiting valve of sorts or even as a possible energy receiver. Tapping into, you guessed it, *Universal Intelligence.* If this is indeed the case, then it is safe to assume that this aspect of our personality survives the death of the body. Personally, it's my view that *mind, consciousness, spirit, soul, and ghost*, are all different words describing the same thing.

It's this exciting research and that of many others which may find the common ground between the ghost hunter and academic scientist that has been eluding us for so long. The real answers we all seek may be right around the corner. Or they may still be years, even generations away.

Thankfully, we have come very far since the Fox Sisters began holding their seances in Rochester New York during the Victorian era. Paranormal research and Parapsychology are no longer just collections of ghost stories in a dusty tome on the library shelf. But a viable science in and of themselves. Creative minds are currently at work developing new and better ITC devices to bridge the gap between here and the hereafter. Mediums and Psychics have come to the forefront of society and are no longer shunned by the masses. But now accepted as messengers who can see beyond the veil.

Till next we meet...

And so we come to the conclusion of this chapter in the career of *Gallo Family Ghost Hunters*. And as readers from all walks of the paranormal spectrum reach this point of the book, I can imagine one of two things happening.

1. **A new group of paranormal enthusiasts have been born.** Those who have read the entirety of this book with an open mind and put together the pieces of the ghostly puzzle provided, realize that there is no other conclusion that can be drawn; ghosts exist, and we have communicated with them.

2. **Skeptics have ripped every last hair from their collective heads**. And that's fine too (well, not that they've made themselves bald that is). Whether you are a paranormal investigator who is skeptical of our theories, equipment, or methodology. Or an outright rationalist who doesn't buy any of it, it's all good!

"To one who has faith, no explanation is necessary. To one without faith, no explanation is possible" -Saint Thomas Aquinas.

We're not talking about blind faith here. The faith we are referring to, is the faith in the evidence we have collected. Because without hard-core scientific proof (whatever that is), most of this endeavor is still theoretical and based on personal experience. So if you don't accept what you see before you, no amount of debate will ever convince you. And as I have stated in the beginning of this book, personal experience is still the best teacher when it comes to ghost hunting.

Finally, I would ask the skeptical reader, *"Do you think, I mean really think that it is remotely possible for every single piece of evidence we have gathered (and you have been presented with scores) to be hallucination, group think, dust, lens flare, pareidolia, imagination, wishful thinking, or whatever? "* Please keep in mind that all it takes is merely *a single piece of evidence to be authentic.* That's right, just one, and we have done our jobs. We have proven the existence of the afterlife and all of the ramifications that come with that discovery. But to be perfectly honest, from our perspective, we have already proven it again and again.

This field is an ever evolving collection of theories, experiments, and methods. Some work, some don't. Even the most well thought out, logical, and well designed equipment sometimes fails miserably. While something you would never expect to work, garners mountains of evidence. Once again, I will state ad nauseam that there are no experts, including us. However, we believe what we believe, and by actual field experience, we know what we know.

A last word about the spirits we have contacted

While what we do is fascinating and can even be thrilling at times, it's still serious business. Ghosts are here for reasons we sometimes cannot fathom and the last thing we want to do is use their gracious allowance of contact to be something we take for granted. These people have stories to tell, and some may be in need of help. Perhaps someday we will learn how to help them; or perhaps that isn't our job at all. The bottom line is this; somehow, they are allowed to communicate with us, albeit in a limited way, and we must make the most of that gift in the most respectful way possible.

I would like to think that books like this give the reader a greater understanding that we live in an amazing and unlimited universe. Filled with wonders, mysteries, and endless possibilities. If this gives someone a little more faith in what happens after death, then that's a good thing. If it stimulates curiosity and a thirst for history and the human condition, great! If you simply enjoyed spending time and ghost hunting right along side of us, then our work is complete.

Thanks for joining us... We love you!

Afterword

I am a skeptic. For me, that means I neither believe nor disbelieve anything until proof is presented for either side. I have considered Bobby a friend of mine for many years now. Yes...sometimes he aggravates me with the orb thing (LOL!), but at the end of the day, he has his opinions, I have mine, and we get along just fine!

Bobby has an infectious enthusiasm for whatever he is doing, but especially when it comes to ghost hunting. He inspires me to get out there and enjoy ghost hunting just for the sake of it. I enjoyed every episode of Gallo Family Ghost Hunters, and if you haven't seen the show, fear not, there is an overview of the best episodes right here.

Bobby writes this book from the point of view of a believer, but he also supplies us alternative explanations of paranormal phenomena to consider, and as a skeptic, I really appreciate that. Family Spirits gives us a great overlook of the history of ghosts, ghost research, ghost communications, and the religious and scientific beliefs centered around these subjects. It is also a good beginners guide to ghost hunting techniques, and the tools currently in use by modern ghost hunters. Regardless of where you stand on the believer-skeptic-disbeliever scale, I think you will find jewels of wisdom and much food for thought in the pages of this book.

April Abercrombie
Paranormal Investigator and Founder of Ghost Advice

Recommended Resources

1. Broome, Fiona. *Ghost Hunting In Haunted Cemeteries.* New Forest Books, 2009.
2. Broome, Fiona. *Ghosts, What they are and what they Aren't.* New Forest Books, 2014.
3. Broome, Fiona. *101 Ghost Hunting Questions Answered.* New Forest Books, 2014.
4. Broome, Fiona., Cote, Rue Taylor. *Ghost Hunting in Tilton, New Hampshire.* CreateSpace Independent Publishing Platform; January 21, 2018.
5. Sweet, Leonore. *How To Photograph The Paranormal.* Hampton Roads Publishing Company, 2005.
6. Heinemann, Klause., ledwith, Miceal. *The Orb Project.* Atria Books/Beyond Words. 2007.
7. Heinemann, Klause. *Orbs Their Meanings and Messages of Hope.* Hay House Inc., 2010.
8. Lanza, Robert., Berman, Bob. *Biocentrism.* BenBella Books; May 18, 2010.
9. Lanza, Robert., Berman, Bob. *Beyond Biocentrism.* BenBella Books; May 2, 2017.
10. Guggenheim, Bill., Guggenheim Judy. *Hello from Heaven.* Random House Publishing Group; March 3, 1997.
11. Booth, John. *Psychic Paradoxes.* Prometheus Books, 1984.
12. Burger, Eugene. *Spirit Theater.* Kaufman and Greenberg, 1986.
13. Houdini, Harry. *Houdini on Magic.* Dover Publications; June 1, 1953.

14. Pearce, Jamie. *Historic Haunts Florida.* Historic Haunts Investigations. First Printing 2011.

15. Stavely, John F. *Ghosts and Gravestones in St. Augustine Florida.* Historic Tours of America, 2005.

16. Roberts, Nancy., Roberts, Bruce. *Illustrated Guide to Ghosts.* Castle Books. 1979 .

17. Kirkpatrick, Cyrus. *Understanding Life After Death.* Developed Life Books; September 6, 2015.

18. Alexander, Eben. *Proof of Heaven.* Simon & Schuster; October 23, 2012.

19. Van Praagh, James. *Ghosts Among Us.* HarperOne; June 16, 2009.

Gallo Family Ghost Hunters Official Channel:
www.GhostHunter.ws

Recommended Ghost Hunting Equipment Source:
www.GhostGear.info

For additional copies of Family Spirits
http://www.FamilySpiritsBook.com

Investigation Photo Albums, Forums, and Additional Videos
https://www.facebook.com/IcomParanormal/

Instagram - Because Nicky G. and Courtnee said so:
https://www.instagram.com/gallofamilygh/

The International Conservatory of Magic Online
www.MagicSchool.com

Fiona Broome's Official Ghost Hunting Website:
www.HollowHill.com

Some celebrities have a star on the Hollywood Walk of Fame... G.F.G.H have a brick embedded in the front walkway of a haunted theater... Ours is much cooler.

NO GHOSTS WERE HARMED
DURING THE WRITING OF THIS BOOK

About the Author

Bobby J. Gallo has been interested in all things weird since a very young age. A modern day *renaissance man*, Bobby is a world class professional magician who has toured the country; performing for colleges, resorts, trade shows, and television audiences. He is also an avid ghost hunter, published author, speaker, networking leader, corporate trainer, web series producer, and musician. Additionally, he is co-creator and headmaster of the *International Conservatory of Magic*... The world's largest online school for magicians.

However, his most important accomplishment by far has been raising his two incredibly talented ghost hunting daughters Nicolet and Courtnee. And has been married for over two decades to his wonderfully patient, and beautiful wife Renee. They reside in *Castello Gallo*, a haunted Italianate brick castle in Roseto Pennsylvania.

You can connect with me on:

- http://www.ghosthunter.ws
- http://twitter.com/BobbyJGallo
- http://www.facebook.com/IcomParanormal
- http://www.ghostgear.info
- http://www.magicschool.com
- http://www.familyspiritsbook.com

Subscribe to my newsletter:

- https://reedsy.com/author/bobby-j-gallo